C0-CCE-533

# UNEMPLOYMENT

## *Its Scope, Measurement, and Effect on Poverty*

*by*

## Robert H. Ferguson

BULLETIN 53-2

MAY 1965

NEW YORK STATE SCHOOL OF INDUSTRIAL AND LABOR RELATIONS, CORNELL UNIVERSITY, ITHACA, NEW YORK

## *About the Author*

ROBERT H. FERGUSON is professor in the Department of Labor Economics and Income Security of the New York State School of Industrial and Labor Relations, where he teaches courses in the economics of wages and employment.

A graduate of Union College, Professor Ferguson received his M. A. degree from Brown University and the Ph. D. degree from Cornell University. A faculty member of the School of Industrial Relations since 1945, he has also taught at the University of Leicester (England) and the University of Rochester. His research interests are in wage determination and problems of unemployment and poverty.

HD
5724
F43

# Contents

# List of Tables

# I

# *The Specter at the Banquet*

*quote*

/ "Unemployment is our number one economic problem. It
wastes the lives of men and women, depriving both them
and the Nation." President John F. Kennedy \

THE YEARS since World War II have been a period of economic
growth and prosperity in which the number of jobs and the level
of incomes in the United States have reached unprecedented heights.
Over 70 million persons are working today, and over half of the
nation's families enjoy incomes exceeding $6,000 a year. An increase
of more than 85 percent since 1947 in the output of goods and services
has produced such an abundance of housing, food, motor cars, home
appliances, and other items that the United States has been labeled
"The Affluent Society."

Yet, at this banquet of plentiful jobs and high incomes, a pathetic
figure lurks in the background, hungry and ill-fed — the specter of
four million Americans looking for, but unable to find, work. Since
1957, the unemployment rate in the United States has stayed at over
5 percent, indicating that more than one in every twenty persons in
the labor force has been jobless.

Unemployment is not a new phenomenon in the American scene, of
course. Whenever the country has suffered a business depression,
large-scale unemployment has appeared. Older persons can never
forget the 1930's, when for ten years one in every five workers was
unemployed and, at the worst, nearly 13 million persons — a fourth
of the work force — were jobless. Even in periods of good business
conditions, some unemployment has always existed. In the years
of prosperity from 1900 to 1929, the rate of unemployment averaged
4.0 percent. In the prosperous years between 1947 and 1957, unemployment averaged 3.4 percent of the labor force.

## REASONS FOR CONCERN

While unemployment is not unusual, today's unemployment is a matter of serious concern for several reasons. There has been a steady growth of joblessness in years of prosperity. From 2.5 percent of the labor force in 1953, unemployment rose to 4.3 percent in 1957, 5.6 percent in 1960, and 5.7 percent in 1963, each a year of high business activity. In 1964, continued prosperity and a tax cut designed to stimulate employment did reduce the rate of unemployment, but only to 5.2 percent. Thus, although the economy has been operating at a high level, it has been unable to provide jobs for all who seek them.

Yet in the next decade, an even larger number of jobs will be needed, for there will be a sharp increase in the number of new workers. Between 1957 and 1964, the labor force grew by less than 900,000 persons annually; between 1964 and 1970 it is expected to increase by 1.5 million persons a year. This means that some 9 million jobs—1.5 million a year—must be created just to take care of new entrants into the job market. Between 1947 and 1963 the average yearly increase in jobs was less than half this amount. Only in 1964, with the special stimulus provided by a tax cut, did the economy yield 1.5 million new jobs. Whether this number of new jobs will be forthcoming in future years remains to be seen.

Popular doubt that employment growth will be maintained at a high enough level is reflected in widespread concern over the elimination of jobs by "automation"—that is, by new machines and methods of production. As the pace of research and invention increases, substitution of mechanical for human workers may take place at an even faster rate.

Another reason for concern about unemployment is the severe hardship it imposes upon the least privileged members of our society—the poorly educated and unskilled, many of whom are Negroes. Even if an adequate number of new jobs is forthcoming in the next decade, these will require skills which can be acquired only by education now unavailable to many individuals.

## HOW MUCH UNEMPLOYMENT?

What is an "acceptable" amount of unemployment? It well might be argued that no unemployment should be tolerated; everyone able and willing to work should be able to find a job. In practice, however, zero unemployment would be impossible to achieve, and, as a matter of fact, it would be undesirable. Some amount of unemployment must exist in a free economy as the consequence of the freedom of workers to quit jobs they do not like and of employers to discharge unneeded or unwanted workers. New persons are continuously entering the labor market looking for work. Others are discharged from or quit old jobs. It takes time for these people to locate new jobs. Likewise, the situation of employers is continually changing. Old businesses contract the size of their operations or shut down. Other firms start up or expand the scale of their operations. These actions produce changes in labor requirements which do not take place simultaneously and instantaneously. Thus the time required for workers to move between jobs creates what is termed "frictional unemployment." Other workers are employed in seasonally active industries, such as highway and building construction, canneries, resort hotels. In the slack seasons these workers either remain unemployed or move into other kinds of work. In any case, they too contribute to the total of "normal" unemployment. It is estimated that so-called normal unemployment approximates 3 percent of the labor force, or an average of about 2¼ million persons.

The President's Council of Economic Advisers, however, does not regard 3 percent as an attainable target for the United States. It feels that 4 percent is a reasonable goal and that efforts to push the rate below 4 percent may result in serious inflation.

## Number of Jobs Needed

The "unemployment problem" thus might be regarded as the task of reducing unemployment from its current level of over 5 percent to 4 percent, a task at present of creating 750,000 more jobs. The matter involves, however, considerably more than this number of additional jobs. Some 2.5 million persons presently work part-time for economic reasons; that is, because they cannot find full-time work. Their unwanted idle time amounts to the equivalent of nearly a million man-years of work, which should be supplied to provide the equivalent of "full employment." As noted earlier, 1.5 million jobs are required for the new entrants into the work force and another 2 million jobs to replace those lost each year from technological change. Nor is this all, for it is estimated that at least 800,000 persons not now looking for work would enter the labor force if job opportunities expanded. Thus, totaling all of these job needs reveals an "unemployment gap" of 6 million jobs which must be filled if unemployment one year hence is to be reduced to the 4 percent level (which would still mean an average unemployment of 3 million persons). In each subsequent year, even with no changes in the rate of labor force growth or displacement of workers by technological advance, 3.5 million new jobs a year will be needed to keep unemployment down to the 4 percent level.

## REASONS FOR UNEMPLOYMENT

What is the reason for the current high level of unemployment? Two principal explanations are offered. One blames unemployment on an inadequate rate of economic growth, due to insufficient consumer demand and business investment. Purchases of goods and services by consumers are not large enough to keep productive facilities fully engaged; therefore, investment in new business and expansion of production are limited, with the result that few new jobs are created. What is needed to increase employment opportunities is increased spending and investment.

The alternative explanation is that structural changes in the economy are responsible for unemployment. These changes comprise a variety of kinds: technological, industrial, occupational, geographical. Rapid technological advance is perhaps the most important factor in transforming the industrial structure. It manifests itself primarily in the form of new machines and tools, new production techniques, and new or improved products. These technological advances have reduced the amount of labor needed to produce nearly all kinds of goods. Farm output, for example, is at an all-time high, but the number of persons employed in agriculture has been rapidly diminishing. Mining and transportation show similar trends. Mining has lost over 350,000 jobs since 1947 and transportation, due to the decline of railroads, has lost 265,000 jobs. Employment growth in recent years has been occurring almost entirely in industries providing services: government; wholesale and retail trade; recreation and amusements; finance, insurance, and real estate; and medicine. These changes have not only reduced the number of jobs in the goods-producing sector of the economy, but have also made it extremely difficult for the displaced workers to find employment in the expanding industries such as education, medicine, and business services, which have different and higher skill requirements.

Even within the goods-producing industries, especially manufacturing, it is the highly skilled occupations which are expanding employment, while the semiskilled and unskilled positions are declining in numbers. A similar occupational shift is occurring throughout the economy. In industry after industry, new jobs are opening for trained workers, while low-skilled jobs are disappearing. Manual workers are becoming an ever smaller proportion of the nation's work force. Since

4

1947, new white-collar jobs have accounted for almost 90 percent of the total employment increase of about 12.5 million jobs.

Industrial changes also have involved significant shifts in the location of business activity, both within and between regions of the country. Many plants have located in suburbs, small cities and villages, even in the open country, to avoid the congestion and high costs of the large cities. New firms and many old ones have located their plants in the newly expanding sections of the country, such as the South and the Far West. Many localities have experienced a decline of local industry because of depletion of resources, such as timber or iron ore. Others have lost jobs as the market for the product of local industry has dwindled, such as the anthracite towns of Pennsylvania. New England has seen over many years the removal of its once-large textile industry to the South. Thus, industrial change has left in its wake many "distressed areas," without sufficient employment for their populations and with little prospect of attracting new industries.

According to those who attribute unemployment primarily to "structural" factors such as described above, programs to increase total consumer spending and business investment are limited in the amount they can accomplish in reducing unemployment due to these causes. Emphasis must be placed, rather, on programs of industrial redevelopment designed to meet the problems of particular communities and areas and on improved employment services and training programs to locate jobs for individual workers and equip them with the necessary skills to hold these jobs.

## WHICH EXPLANATION IS CORRECT?

The difference of opinion between those who argue that an inadequate rate of growth is responsible for unemployment and those who maintain that unemployment is mainly a structural affair is significant but should not be exaggerated. In government circles, it is primarily the President's Council of Economic Advisers and the Treasury Department which have supported the inadequate growth-rate thesis, while the Department of Labor and the Federal Reserve officials have emphasized the structural argument. In business and labor circles, both ideas have wide support.

The two explanations of unemployment, within limits, complement rather than conflict with each other. In a more rapidly growing economy, old jobs would disappear more slowly and new jobs would open up more quickly and in larger number, thus easing the difficulties of workers in changing employment. Employers would be less stringent in hiring standards and more willing to spend time and money in

5

training new workers, while workers would have a greater choice of positions. On the other hand, a more flexible economy — in which displaced workers received assistance in locating, training for, and moving to new jobs — would benefit from an enhanced pace of growth without risking the danger of inflation.

This bulletin attempts nothing so ambitious as trying to determine the reasons for the persistence of a high level of unemployment. Rather, it explores other less difficult, but equally important, aspects of the unemployment problem. Why is the unemployment situation a matter of national concern? How do we measure the amount of joblessness in the economy? Who are the persons who are seeking, but not finding, work? Is unemployment a widespread condition in the United States or does it affect some categories of persons more than others? Is being without a job simply that, or are there different kinds of unemployment, some more serious to the person concerned and to society than others? How is unemployment related to poverty?

# II

# *Does Everyone Need a Job?*

> "...it is the continuing policy and responsibility of the
> Federal Government...to promote maximum employment,
> production, and purchasing power."
>
> Employment Act of 1946

WHY ARE we, as a nation, so concerned about unemployment?
People without jobs scarcely constitute a new problem, nor is the
present amount of unemployment, as was noted in Chapter I, especially high as compared with earlier years.

To some extent, our concern with unemployment may result simply
from the attention paid to the government's monthly statistics on
employment by the press and radio. Even relatively minor changes in
employment and unemployment are the subjects of analysis and
comment. In the absence of the detailed statistics issued from Washington, many persons would be unaware, perhaps, of the existence of
any unemployment in our economy. Although as a nation we may
have become too "statistics conscious" in recent years, this tendency
alone could not possibly account for the intensity of our interest in
the job problem. There are more fundamental reasons why unemployment is an issue of national concern.

## AUTOMATION

Most publicized of the various reasons for worry about employment
are fears about "automation." While technological change involving
the replacement of men by machines has always been going on, there
is today widespread anxiety that the rate at which machines are
taking over work formerly performed by people is soaring and that
the day of the "automatic factory" may arrive in the near future.
While everyone agrees that new machines and new processes create,
as well as destroy, jobs, there is genuine worry that new jobs are
not being provided as fast as old ones disappear. Equally a cause of

7

concern for many persons is the fact that the new jobs brought into being by "automation" are largely in different industries, occupations, and geographical areas than the jobs which are disappearing. Although the development of space missiles may open up hundreds of jobs for electronics technicians in Florida, this does not help the coal miner in West Virginia who has been replaced by a new digging machine. The actual rate at which new machines and methods of production are pushing men and women out of jobs is not known, but government estimates put it at 2 million persons per year. There thus is concern that in some part present unemployment reflects a situation which may worsen drastically if research and invention increase the pace of technological innovation.

A high rate of unemployment used to be considered the result of poor business conditions, a phenomenon which would disappear when business improved. A major source of concern about unemployment in recent years, however, has been its high level in years of prosperity, a level, as earlier noted, which has been increasing since the Korean War. Is this the result of "automation"? Many persons think that it is, pointing to industries which have greatly expanded their output over the past decade although they employ fewer workers now than ten years ago. The motor vehicle industry is an example. Production of cars and trucks increased by over 2.5 million vehicles (nearly 40 percent) between 1954 and 1963, but the industry employed 54,000 fewer workers in the latter year. Not all economists, however, regard the persistence of considerable unemployment in prosperous times to be the result of automation. These analysts, who include the President's Council of Economic Advisers, believe that consumer purchasing power, and therefore the demand for goods and services, has not been growing at a fast enough pace to use the nation's productive capacity and manpower fully. The failure of demand to increase rapidly enough they attribute to faults in our tax structure and other factors. If consumer demand were strong enough, it is argued, workers now displaced by new techniques would be able to find other work in the same or different industries.

It is not just our inability to reduce the present amount of unemployment, however, which causes great concern. Over the next ten years the number of persons seeking jobs will be increasing by 1.5 million annually, nearly twice the rate of the last half dozen years, during which we have been unable to reduce unemployment significantly. If joblessness is not to increase, the economy must do far better in creating new employment opportunities than it has done in recent years.

8

# POVERTY: ONE-FIFTH OF THE NATION

Our concern over unemployment does not arise, however, simply from the present or potential future numbers of jobless persons. It can be argued that there is nothing alarming about the present amount of unemployment, that our concern only reflects a greater sensitivity to the plight of the jobless. Whether or not this argument is correct, it is true that interest in reducing unemployment is not simply a "matter of numbers." Indeed, statistics on the number of jobless merely describe the magnitude of unemployment; they do not indicate why it is a "problem."

The foremost factor underlying our anxiety about unemployment is worry about the economic deprivation which may be suffered by the person without work and his family. Unemployment, whether temporary or long-run, is a principal cause of poverty. In announcing that he was "declaring unconditional war on poverty in America" in his 1964 State of the Union Message, President Lyndon B. Johnson pointed out that 35 million Americans were living at or below the boundaries of poverty — nearly one-fifth of the nation.

At first glance, unemployment would not seem to be a major cause of poverty, for only 5 percent of the heads of the 8.8 million poor families in the United States in 1963 were reported in the official statistics as "unemployed." Closer analysis reveals, however, lack of adequate employment to be most important as a reason for poverty. Less than half of the heads of these poor families had jobs; while only 5 percent were unemployed, some 48 percent were "not in the labor force"; that is, they were jobless but not actively seeking work. A substantial number of these persons were unable to work, of course, because of old age, poor health, and other personal characteristics. Many of them, however, were not seeking work because they knew, or felt fairly certain, that they could not find work. In 32 percent of these poor families, there were no earners at all. In only 24 percent were two or more persons working, in contrast to the presence of two or more wage earners in 45 percent of the families in better circumstances.

## THE "WAR ON POVERTY"

The chief aim of the war on poverty is to improve employment opportunities for the economically deprived individuals in the nation by (1) developing resources and businesses in the "distressed areas" so as to provide more jobs, and (2) improving the educational and skill levels of the underprivileged so that they may qualify for good jobs which will provide them adequate incomes.

9

The position of the Negro in American society is an important part of our national concern with poverty and unemployment. In 1963, according to federal government data, 43 percent of all Negro families were "poor" — that is, receiving less than $3,000 in annual income, as contrasted with 16 percent of white families. The average income of white families is nearly twice that of Negro families. Racial discrimination and poor education not only prevent Negroes from entering higher paying occupations but also restrict them to types of jobs where unemployment is high. The rate of unemployment of Negroes is twice that of whites, Negroes losing their jobs more often and remaining without work longer than whites. Accordingly, improvement of employment opportunities is a basic need if there is to be real improvement in the Negro's situation in the United States.

A vital reason for public interest in mitigating unemployment and poverty is the belief that these twin evils have no place in a society as rich and productive as the United States. Since the great depression of the 1930's, persons of all political beliefs agree that unemployment is an economic and social disaster, which the government must combat with every weapon at its command. This national resolve was embodied in law at the end of World War II in the Employment Act of 1946, which states that

...it is the continuing policy and responsibility of the Federal Government to use all practicable means consistent with its needs and obligations and other essential considerations of national policy, with the assistance and cooperation of industry, agriculture, labor, and State and local governments, to coordinate and utilize all its plans, functions, and resources for the purpose of creating and maintaining, in a manner calculated to foster and promote free competitive enterprise and the general welfare, conditions under which there will be afforded useful employment, for those able, willing, and seeking to work, and to promote maximum employment, production, and purchasing power.

## THE EMPLOYMENT ACT OF 1946

The Employment Act provides that the President at the start of each year shall transmit an "Economic Report" to the Congress "setting forth the levels of employment, production, and purchasing power obtaining in the United States and such levels needed to carry out" the policy of the act. In addition to reviewing the economic program of the federal government and economic conditions generally in the country as they affect employment, the President is required to submit a program for achieving maximum employment and the other objectives set out in the act.

In preparing his Economic Report, the President is assisted by a Council of Economic Advisers, consisting of three economists who working with professional aides, consultants, and other government agencies, are responsible for making studies and reports on national economic conditions.

The Joint Economic Committee of the Congress, comprised of eight Senators and eight Representatives, conducts hearings on the President's Economic Report — at which professional economists, government officials, and spokesmen from business, agriculture, and labor are invited to present their ideas and opinions, — and then issues its own report. The committee, which employs a small professional staff of its own, also conducts studies and hearings on a variety of specific topics related to the national economic welfare, ranging from the balance of payments in foreign trade to the causes of poverty.

Other congressional committees also have conducted investigations of employment problems in recent years. One of the most extensive studies was that of the Special Committee on Unemployment Problems of the Senate in 1959–1960. The Senate Committee on Labor and Public Welfare and the House Committee on Education and Labor have conducted an almost continuous series of hearings on various aspects of unemployment. As a result of these hearings, Congress has enacted the Manpower Development and Training Act, the Area Redevelopment Act, the Public Works Acceleration Act, and other measures designed to aid in meeting unemployment problems.

## Earlier Neglect of Unemployment

Governmental concern with the problem of unemployment is of recent origin, however, from a historical viewpoint. Business panics, depressions, and widespread joblessness were frequent occurrences in the nineteenth century and in the first three decades of the twentieth, but scant notice was paid by government to the privation, debt, hunger, and suffering of the jobless, and little attention was directed to possible measures to prevent business downturns. Help for the unemployed was left to local, usually private, charities, and suggestions that the national government take steps to deal with business depressions were condemned as interference with the "natural economic laws" of free enterprise.

As Stephen Bailey has pointed out in his history of the Employment Act of 1946,

It is not, in fact, an exaggeration to say that the great depression of the 1930's was the first occasion in our nation's history when the federal government took active and positive steps to alleviate widespread economic suffering, and undertook to use its offices to harness destructive economic forces and to establish institutional mechanisms for protecting the individual against economic disaster.[1]

The enormity of the economic collapse in the 1930's forced the federal government to undertake large-scale programs to aid the unemployed and equally unprecedented action to stimulate economic recovery. Whatever views might have been previously entertained about the propriety of "government intervention," it was universally recognized that only the federal government had the power to do anything really effective about the disastrous economic situation confronting the United States.

The New Deal programs for aiding the unemployed and promoting business recovery were an amalgam of enthusiasm, improvisation, and inconsistency. How effective they were remains a matter of controversy. As late as 1940, over 8 million persons (15 percent of the labor force) still were jobless. Nonetheless, these New Deal projects and the concept of government responsibility for the economic welfare of the nation embodied in them symbolized a change in American economic and political philosophy of tremendous importance.

## WARTIME DEVELOPMENTS

The entrance of the United States into World War II virtually eliminated unemployment, as the nation strained to meet the demands on production and manpower imposed by the conflict. Concern about unemployment did not disappear, however, for the question was widely asked, "What will happen after the war ends?" Fearful that the war had only temporarily removed the causes of economic difficulty, many individuals, businessmen, union leaders, and government officials anticipated the possibility of a sharp rise in unemployment with the cessation of production for the military, the resumption of economic activity in Europe, and the return of servicemen to civilian life. Opinions on the course of action which should be undertaken varied widely.

Many, perhaps most, businessmen felt that economic stability and full employment could be achieved only by providing the maximum of freedom and encouragement to private enterprise. In essence, this meant low taxes and a minimum of government regulation of business. Some business leaders, however, particularly members of the newly formed Committee for Economic Development, believed that some kinds of government programs and "economic planning" would aid the attainment of economic stability.

---

[1]Stephen K. Bailey, *Congress Makes a Law* (New York: Columbia University Press, 1950), p. 5.

Labor union officials, on the other hand, contended that the government had a basic responsibility to assure the maintenance of full employment. In their opinion, this involved not only the usual sorts of measures advocated by unions, such as higher minimum wages and improved unemployment compensation, but also advance planning of public works programs and other measures to counteract the effects of business recessions.

In the federal government itself, the need for consideration of the economic problems which might confront the country after the war was early recognized. By mid-1943, a dozen or more federal agencies were engaged in drawing up economic plans for the postwar period. In Congress, there was similar concern and activity. The Senate created a Special Committee on Postwar Economic Policy and Planning in March 1943. During 1943 and 1944, this and other committees gave extensive consideration both to the immediate problems which would be involved in the termination of military production and to the desirability of a permanent government program for coping with depressions and unemployment.

At the same time, the notion of government's responsibility for providing full employment entered the presidential campaign of 1944, although not as a controversial issue, for both parties included it in their platforms. While the Democrats promised action to "guarantee full employment and provide prosperity," the Republicans stated "we shall promote the fullest stable employment through private enterprise." Although the G. O. P. rejected "the theory of restoring prosperity through government spending and deficit financing," endorsement of the concept of government responsibility to provide jobs by the party traditionally strongly opposed to "government intervention" indicated a major turning point in political philosophy.[2]

## FULL EMPLOYMENT BILL

In January 1945, a Full Employment Bill was introduced in the Senate.

The Full Employment Bill, as introduced, attempted to do four things: first, to establish once and for all the principle of the "right to work" and the federal government's obligation to assure employment opportunities for all those "able to work and seeking work"; second, to place responsibility on the President for seeing to it that the economy was purposively analyzed at regular intervals, and that the Congress was informed of economic trends and of the President's program to meet the challenge of those trends; third, in case the economic barometer read "stormy," to commit the federal government to undertake a series of measures to forestall serious economic diffi-

[2]*Ibid.*, pp. 41–43.

culty — the measure of last resort being a program of federal spending and investment which was to be the final guarantor of full employment; and finally, to establish a mechanism in Congress which would facilitate legislative analysis and action, and fix legislative responsibility for the carrying out of a full employment policy.[3]

Members of Congress, particularly those who were conservative in their economic beliefs, were not prepared, however, to accept the extent of government control of economic activity suggested in the bill, which authorized the President to recommend a program for combating unemployment which might "include, but need not be limited to,...activities with reference to banking and currency, monopoly and competition, wages and working conditions, foreign trade and investment, agriculture, taxation, social security, the development of natural resources, and such other matters as may directly or indirectly affect the level of non-Federal investment and expenditures."[4] Nor were they sympathetic to the idea that the government should increase its own expenditures whenever it appeared likely that the volume of private spending and investment would be inadequate to maintain economic activity at the full-employment level. The theory of "deficit spending" — that is, the government deliberately spending more than its revenues in order to pump additional money into the economy — was far from accepted as good economics in 1945, despite the widespread discussion of the idea which had gone on since the mid-1930's.

As the consequence of opposition to "economic planning," "deficit spending," and "government intervention," the employment bill finally approved by Congress in 1946 was far different in nature from the bill originally introduced in January 1945. It constituted, in effect, no more than a statement of policy; namely, that it is a responsibility of the federal government to promote full employment. The Employment Act of 1946 provided, through the President's Economic Report, the Council of Economic Advisers, and the Joint Economic Committee, a continuously functioning arrangement for focusing the spotlight of public attention on the issue of employment, but what kind of action, if any, the government should take to combat business recession and unemployment was not suggested.

## What Is Maximum Employment?

In the area of economics and politics, however, even a relatively simple statement of policy may arouse disagreement and controversy. Such has been the case with Section 2 of the Employment Act. What

---

[3]*Ibid.*, pp. 13–14.
[4]Full Employment Act of 1946, 79th Cong., 1st sess., S. 380, §3 (b).

loes the phrase "promote maximum employment" mean? Should everyone who wishes to work be provided with a job? Should the government be concerned with the inability of teen-age students or married women to find employment or should attention be given only to the needs of heads of families? Is there some minimum amount of unemployment that is "normal" for the economy? If so, is it 2 percent 3 percent, 5 percent of the labor force?

Neither economists nor politicians have been able to reach agreement on a definition of "full employment." The political basis for this lack of agreement is fairly easy to explain. The tighter the definition of full employment — that is, the closer it comes to demanding that everyone be provided full-time work at all times — the more continuous and intensive must be government activities in the economic field. The looser the definition — that is, the greater the amount of unemployment accepted as "normal" and therefore not a matter of concern — the less frequently will the government be required to take action. It is not surprising, therefore, to find that persons who believe the government should intervene in economic affairs where necessary — for example, enacting minimum wage laws, providing medical care for the elderly, regulating business practices, etc. — are unwilling to accept as "normal" as large an amount of unemployment as those who oppose a system of "guided capitalism under government planners."

The disagreement among economists over the definition of "full employment" arises, however, from technical considerations rather than conflicting political beliefs. All economists agree that some amount of unemployment is both normal and desirable in a free economic system. New workers are continually entering the job market searching for employment. While in this process of locating satisfactory jobs, they are counted as "unemployed." Experienced workers, for a variety of reasons but chiefly to improve their earnings, give up old jobs and look for new ones. In the interim, they too are "unemployed." Other workers, and these make up the largest group, have been laid off by their employers because of declining business or technical changes that have reduced the firm's need for labor. At the same time, other firms, expanding in size because of new and improved products or lower prices, need additional workers. It takes time, however, for the discharged worker to locate a position with one of the latter firms and during this period he is counted as "unemployed." Finally, many industries are "seasonal" in the pattern of their operations: their level of activity fluctuates with the time of year. Building construction and resort hotels, for example, employ many more workers in summer than in winter. Workers in these industries may be counted as "unemployed" during the slack seasons or while they are searching for work in other industries. Closely allied to the "seasonally unemployed" are workers in industries like longshoring, some kinds of manufacturing, and mining where work load and employment fluctuate continuously.

## THE ECONOMISTS' DILEMMA

Unemployment arising for the reasons described above is unavoidable if individuals are to be permitted freedom of choice in finding jobs and changing employers and if business firms are to be free to adapt to changing economic conditions. The economist's dilemma arises from the necessity of deciding what proportion of existing unemployment is due to this normal movement of workers into and out of the labor market and between jobs and what proportion is due to faulty functioning of the economy. It is the latter kind of unemployment, resulting from the failure of the economy to provide enough jobs for everyone, rather than the unemployment associated with persons shifting from one job to another, that constitutes the true "unemployment problem."

Unfortunately, it is not an easy matter to come up with even a rough, let alone a precise, estimate of the amount of "normal" unemployment. Existing methods of gathering data on unemployment do not provide information on reasons for unemployment, nor is it likely that techniques for doing so can easily be devised. It is possible to identify new job-seekers who have not worked previously, and seasonal unemployment is estimated by extremely crude techniques, but this is about all. Consequently, if 4,500,000 persons, representing approximately 6 percent of the labor force, are reported as unemployed, it is not possible to say that 2 percent or 3 percent or some other rate constitutes "normal" unemployment.

## "NORMAL" UNEMPLOYMENT

Even more difficult to deal with, however, is the concept of "normal" unemployment itself. As described above, it embraces two groups: (1) persons seeking their first jobs or changing jobs, and (2) employees of seasonal industries or industries where short-term fluctuations in employment levels are customary. The fact that such unemployment exists does not imply that, like death and taxes, it is totally inescapable.

Studies of persons seeking jobs have disclosed that most individuals look for work in a very inefficient fashion. Many are handicapped by inadequate information about existing job opportunities and by lack

16

of "know-how" in applying for a job. Others do not search beyond a very limited geographic area. Some persons lack the money to move to another area where jobs are available. Still others mistakenly cling to the notion that "something will happen" to restore their old jobs and do not vigorously seek new employment. Whatever the reasons for inefficiency in job seeking, it is certain that the "frictional" unemployment it produces could be markedly reduced by an improved and expanded public employment service and better vocational training and guidance in the schools. Some amount of time is required for an individual to locate a new job, but it is not fixed nor irreducible; hence, so-called "normal employment" is not an immutable quantity but rather is dependent upon the amount of effort which the government puts into improving the efficiency of the job market.

Similarly, "seasonal" unemployment and the "casual" unemployment caused by short-term fluctuations in production may be reduced by better planning by business firms. In automobile manufacturing, for example, introduction of the new models of cars in the period when sales normally are slack has done much to smooth out the production schedule in this once highly seasonal industry. In longshoring the number of workers needed on a particular pier varies widely from day to day. Under the traditional "shape-up" system of hiring, workers used to go to each pier in the morning, not knowing whether or not they might find work. If they did not, it was by then too late to look for jobs at other piers. Today, employment is directed through central "hiring halls" managed by the government or unions, and workers are directed to the particular piers where they are needed. Despite the strides made in these and other industries toward smoothing out fluctuations in employment, it is generally recognized that much more still might be done toward this end.

## The Supply of Workers

Difficulties in reaching agreement on what constitutes "normal" employment are not limited to the demand, or job availability, side of the labor market. Equally vexing problems are encountered on the supply side in trying to estimate the desires and characteristics of persons seeking jobs.

Does everyone seeking work actually want a year-round, full-time job? Those who argue against a "tight" definition of full employment point out that a significant number of people want to work only part of the year, while others desire only part-time jobs (less than 35 hours a week). In 1962, for example, some 20 million persons (a fourth of all the people who were employed during the year) worked fewer than fifty weeks for "non-economic" reasons. Many were students who held jobs only in vacation periods, while the other large group consisted of married women whose homemaking obligations kept them out of the job market for part of the year or whose desire for extra income was limited. Part-time workers (those putting in less than 35 hours a week) constituted a fifth of all workers in 1962; three-fourths of these persons, again mainly students and housewives, did not want full-time jobs.

## Secondary Earners

Persons who wish to work only part time or for part of the year are often described as "secondary earners," since with few exceptions their earnings are not adequate to support themselves or their families, but rather supplement the main source of family income, usually the earnings of the husband or father. Secondary earners enter the job market for various reasons. Students take jobs to earn money for college expenses. Wives also may work to help meet the costs of education, to pay family medical bills, to aid in purchase of a new home or automobile. Yet another group of part-year and/or part-time workers includes retired persons who need to supplement their pension income or who work in order "to keep busy."

Considerable controversy exists over the issue of whether inability of such secondary earners to find jobs constitutes an unemployment problem requiring government intervention. According to one point of view, unemployment is significant mainly in so far as it affects heads of families or individuals living alone — that is, primary earners. Secondary earners, it is asserted, are likely to suffer unemployment because they are available only for part-year or part-time work, because they move so frequently into and out of the job market, and because they are mainly low-skilled or untrained. Inclusion of teen-agers and married women inflates the total unemployment figure, it is argued, and exaggerates the seriousness of the problem.

Table 1 presents data for the year 1963 illustrating this contention. Teen-agers contributed nearly 25 percent of the unemployment total, although they represented only 9 percent of the labor force. Young persons 20 to 24 years of age added another 16 percent to the total of jobless, although they were only 10 percent of the labor force. Unemployment is a normal condition in these age groups, it is said, since many are looking for their first jobs and others change jobs frequently in a search for the type of work that suits them. In addition, about 30 percent of those 14 to 24 who are in the labor force are also in school. For them, employment is secondary to education.

*Table 1.* Unemployed Persons by Age and Household
Relationship, 1963.

| Age and Household Relationship | Thousands of Persons | Percent Distribution | Unemployment Rate (%) |
|---|---|---|---|
| *Age* | | | |
| Total | 4,166 | 100.0 | 5.7 |
| 14 to 19 years | 979 | 23.5 | 15.6 |
| 20 to 24 years | 658 | 15.8 | 8.8 |
| 25 to 64 years | 2,401 | 57.6 | 4.3 |
| 65 years and over | 126 | 3.0 | 4.1 |
| *Household Relationship* | | | |
| Total | 4,166 | 100.0 | 5.7 |
| Household head | 1,645 | 39.5 | 3.7 |
| Living with relatives | 1,382 | 33.2 | 3.5 |
| Not living with relatives | 263 | 6.3 | 5.4 |
| Wife of head | 716 | 17.2 | 5.3 |
| Other relative of head | 1,699 | 40.8 | 12.7 |
| Non-relative of head | 105 | 2.5 | 6.7 |

*Source:* U. S. Bureau of Labor Statistics, "Special Labor Force Report No. 43: Labor Force and Employment in 1963," by Susan S. Holland, *Monthly Labor Review,* June 1964, Reprint No. 2442, pp. A-34, A-39.

Table 1 also indicates that the rate of joblessness for family heads ("household heads living with relatives") is much lower than the total unemployment rate or the rates for working wives, relatives, and persons living alone. It is family heads, so it is argued, whose unemployment is a matter of serious concern. This view was reflected in the Full Employment Bill of 1945, which stated:

All Americans able to work and seeking work have the right to useful, remunerative, regular, and full-time employment, and it is the policy of the United States to assure the existence at all times of sufficient employment opportunities to enable all Americans *who have finished their schooling and who do not have full-time housekeeping responsibilities* freely to exercise this right...(italics added).

## EMPLOYMENT FOR ALL PERSONS

Exponents of the opposite view — that all persons seeking jobs should be able to find work — refuse to accept the idea that unemployment of youths, wives, and other secondary earners is either normal or a matter of minor importance.

The Employment Act of 1946, they point out, sets no limitations on who should be provided employment; rather, the act states national policy to be to maintain "conditions under which there will be afforded

19

useful employment, for those able, willing, and seeking work, and to promote maximum employment, production, and purchasing power."

Indeed, maximizing production and purchasing power clearly requires, it is asserted, that full use be made of available manpower and womanpower. No one would argue that the United States is so well supplied with schools, hospitals, good roads, housing, and other facilities or that individuals and families are so well off in terms of food, clothing, and other necessities that no need exists to enlarge the nation's output of goods and services. Reducing the unemployment rate from 5 percent to 4 percent would increase the gross national product by $20 billion, according to the President's Council of Economic Advisers.

Greater employment opportunities are also needed, it is maintained, to provide the incomes for purchasing more goods and services. Emphasis only upon the employment situation of the family head neglects the importance of the contribution to family income made by so-called secondary earners. Employed wives and other family members aid greatly in raising family purchasing power. In 1963, for example, only 24 percent of the nation's poor families had two or more earners; in contrast, nearly half the families with incomes of $3,000 and above had two or more earners in each family. It is evident, therefore, that although the husband may provide the main part of the family income, the earnings of other members may be responsible for the family living at a comfortable level rather than just "scraping along" or actually living in poverty.

Provision of ample job opportunities for all who wish to work is important also, it is asserted, to permit individuals to fulfill their needs for self-expression and creativity. Unmarried girls, for example, or married women with no children at home should not be condemned to idleness and frustration if they have the time and desire to work outside the home.

## Opportunities for Youth

Even more compelling is the argument against regarding the lack of employment opportunities for young persons as unimportant. Teenagers need to acquire knowledge about jobs and the ways of the business world and to develop good work habits and skills. This they can do, however, only by acquiring actual work experience. If a lack of jobs denies them this opportunity, they may lose their initiative and ambition and drift into idleness. Here too, it is pointed out, it is necessary to take into consideration the fact that about half of all boys and girls 16 to 21 years of age do not attend school and therefore, ideally at least, should be working. In fact, however, only about 7 in 10 are in the labor force, and of these youths about 13 percent are unemployed. Even among youths who are full-time high school or college students, employment may be necessary to permit these youngsters to attend school.

Perhaps the most damaging argument against the thesis that the unemployed should be sorted out by age, family status, or school enrollment is the fact that such distinctions are meaningless in the actual creation of job opportunities. It is not possible to create jobs just for male family heads and not for other persons, nor for youths not in school as against those attending school. Employers may discriminate among various categories of persons in filling existing jobs, but government and private efforts to expand the number of jobs cannot be so directed as to create employment for specific groups.

## An Acceptable Level of Unemployment

If the argument that all persons able and willing to work should have opportunity to do so is conceded, what constitutes an acceptable or "normal" level of unemployment? Perhaps the best source of guidance is the Council of Economic Advisers—the government agency responsible for advising the President and the Congress on this question. Interestingly, however, one discovers that only recently has the Council been willing to put forth a definite figure.

In its annual reports for 1947 and 1948, the Council stated that unemployment averaging a little over two million persons (3.9 percent of the labor force) indicated that "aggregate employment was substantially in accord with objectives stated by Congress in the Employment Act." In its subsequent reports, however, the Council offered no estimates of normal unemployment, an omission for which it was criticized by the Joint Economic Committee of the Congress. Testifying before the committee in 1955, the chairman of the Council said: "Although 4 percent of the labor force is nowadays widely regarded as an approximate measure of the amount of frictional and seasonal unemployment, the Council has not favored this or any other rigid figure to serve as a trigger to governmental action or as a measure of good performance."

In 1961, however, under a different President and with a changed membership, the Council did adopt a 4 percent unemployment level as a satisfactory estimate of structural and frictional unemployment and suggested that a rate of 4 percent would constitute an attainable goal of government policy. The following year, President Kennedy stated, "We cannot afford to settle for any prescribed level of unem-

21

ployment. But for working purposes we view a 4 percent unemployment rate as a temporary target." Subsequent *Economic Reports of the President* have continued to speak of an "interim target level of 4 percent."

Events, more than economic theories, probably explain the government's position respecting a definition of full employment. Between 1947 and 1960 the rate of unemployment was below 4.5 percent in eight of these fourteen years. Far more concern was felt about the dangers of inflation, which was seen as the major problem of this period, than about unemployment, which in 1957 was 4.3 percent of the labor force. In 1958, however, the rate rose to 6.8 percent and did not decline through 1963 below 5.5 percent. At the same time, prices ceased their upward course. Thus unemployment loomed as the major economic problem.

Four percent seems to have been chosen as a goal for two reasons. First, only during World War II and the Korean conflict did the rate fall to 3 percent or below. In years of peace, 4 percent has been the lowest rate reached. Second, it has seemed extremely uncertain that starting from a level of 5 percent or higher it would be possible to reduce the rate below 4 percent without taking massive and drastic actions which might rekindle the fires of inflation. Economists who believe that a large part of unemployment is structural in nature contend that only a long program of improved education, retraining of older persons, and area redevelopment can reduce the unemployment rate below 4 percent.

# III

# *How Many Are Unemployed?*

"These statistics are of vital importance as measures of
the economic health and well-being of the Nation."
President John F. Kennedy


IN NEWSPAPER headlines and political oratory, *the* unemployment rate is the total number of jobless persons expressed as a percentage of the civilian labor force. This figure has such political significance that it has been called "the most important single statistic published by the Federal Government." The national unemployment rate is widely accepted as an indicator both of the economic prosperity of the country and of the extent of distress caused by lack of jobs.

To what extent it is valid, however, to attempt to summarize the employment situation of the entire United States by a single figure is open to serious question. Labor union spokesmen have argued that the official figure is too low, failing to reflect the lost hours of work of those employed part time and omitting from the unemployed those who have given up the search for work after fruitless months of job seeking. Some businessmen, on the other hand, contend that the unemployment figure is too high because it includes teen-agers looking for baby-sitting jobs, housewives who do not need to work, temporarily unemployed persons who have a job to return to, and so on. A committee appointed by the President to study these charges has commented that "there is no single definition of labor force or of unemployment which is obviously *the* correct one."

How unemployment should be defined depends upon the purpose for which data on joblessness are desired. The unemployment rate for married men is obviously a better indicator of family hardship than a figure which also includes job-seeking teen-agers and single women. The rate for experienced workers is the best guide to the extent of

23

layoffs, while the rate for 14 to 19 year olds may indicate the relative difficulty faced by new workers in finding jobs. Actually, the federal government publishes a large amount of detailed information on employment and unemployment — by age, sex, occupation, industry, color, marital status, hours worked, and the like — so that most needs for which information is desired can be satisfied.

## EMPLOYMENT STATISTICS

United States statistics on employment and unemployment are the most comprehensive of any country in the world. This information is obtained from three sources: (1) a monthly survey of 35,000 households, conducted by the Bureau of the Census, which provides detailed information on employment and unemployment for the nation as a whole; (2) monthly reports from 180,000 industrial establishments, submitted to the Department of Labor, which provide information on employment, hours, and earnings by industry; and (3) claims filed for unemployment insurance benefits, which provide data on joblessness by localities. The data from these sources are published monthly by the U. S. Department of Labor in *The Monthly Report on the Labor Force* and *Employment and Earnings,* and also appear in magazines and newspapers.

The survey made by the Bureau of the Census is the most important source of information on national employment and unemployment. The 35,000 households visited monthly by highly trained investigators include about 80,000 persons. Located in 357 areas, these households comprise a scientifically selected sample, representative of the population of the country as a whole. Urban and rural areas, different types of industrial and farming areas, and the major geographic divisions of the country are included in the sample in the same proportion as they exist in the nation.

The interviews include about one in every 1,500 households in the country. Each month about one-fourth of the households in the sample are replaced, so that no family is interviewed for more than four months in a row. Although this sample seems extremely small in relation to the total population of the country, statisticians regard the results as highly accurate. The chances are 19 out of 20 that the estimate of unemployment would differ from a complete count by less than 200,000. Since total unemployment has run about 4 to 5 million in recent years, any error in the sample is not large enough to distort significantly the picture of unemployment which it presents.

Unfortunately, although the households in the sample are located

24

in all of the fifty states, it cannot be used to provide information on employment and unemployment by state or locality. The reason is that the accuracy of a sample depends more on the size of the sample itself than on the size of the total population it represents. To obtain information by state would require fifty additional samples, each nearly as large as the single sample now used for the entire country.

The census sample survey was begun in 1940. Prior to that date we have no really accurate data on unemployment. The Bureau of Labor Statistics' monthly series of reports on employment, hours, and earnings by industry, however, began in 1915 and is one of our oldest continuous series of statistics. The BLS collects information monthly from employers on total number of employees, total number of production workers, hours worked by and earnings of production workers. This too is a sample, but a much larger one than the census household sample, including from 16 to 100 percent of the employees in various industries.

The BLS establishment information provides data on number of employees and weekly hours worked in industries at the national, state, and local levels. It does not provide data on unemployment or the detailed information on age, sex, marital status, and other characteristics of workers furnished by the census survey or unemployment insurance claims.

Unemployment insurance claims give detailed information on the personal and occupational characteristics of the unemployed. These data are collected weekly, since the recipient of unemployment benefits must file a claim each week at his local employment office. Because of the localized nature of the operation, these claims provide information on unemployment by state and locality not available from the household survey of the Census Bureau.

Only about two-thirds of all workers are covered by unemployment insurance programs, however, the principal groups excluded being persons in agriculture, domestic service, state and local government, the self-employed, unpaid family workers, and employees of firms below a minimum size. This means that the number of jobless persons reported in unemployment insurance statistics is less than the total reported by the household survey, which covers all persons in the labor force. The two sets of figures may also differ in the event of prolonged unemployment, since the unemployed are dropped from the claims figures after their insurance benefit period has expired. In general, however, the two sets of figures on unemployment follow remarkably parallel courses over time, moving up and down in close harmony.

25

# Who Is Unemployed?

Who is counted as unemployed? Under the unemployment insurance program the answer is clear-cut: an individual drawing benefits, something he can do only if he previously worked, is now without a job, and provides some evidence that he is looking for work. Identification of the unemployed in the census household survey, however, is a more difficult and controversial matter, because the effort to determine the employment status of all persons 14 years of age and over encounters tricky and elusive issues. Should a high-school student unsuccessfully seeking baby-sitting jobs be counted unemployed? How should a man of 67 who "would work if I could find a job" be classified? Is a woman temporarily idle, but with definite assurance of recall to her old job in three weeks, employed or unemployed? Should a skilled machinist working a few hours a week as a gasoline station attendant be considered as employed, or should his inability to find work at his regular occupation classify him as unemployed? Since misunderstanding of the way in which the Census Bureau gathers its information on unemployment frequently arises, it is worthwhile to describe the method by which the Bureau decides whether persons are "employed," "unemployed," or "not in the labor force" (not employed and not looking for work).

A personal interview with a member of each of the 35,000 households in the Census Bureau's sample is the basic source of information. To make sure that all interviews follow the same procedure so that the results will be comparable, and also to avoid relying on the judgments or opinions of the interviewer or person being interviewed, the questions asked are identical in every interview.

In order to determine the employment status of each person 14 years of age or older in each household, the following major questions are asked:

1. What was he (or she) doing most of last week — working, keeping house, going to school, or something else?

For each person who was not working, the next question asked is:

2. Did he do any work at all last week, not counting work around the house?

For the persons for whom the second question was answered no, the next question is:

3. Was he looking for work?

If the answer is no, the next question is:

4. Even though he did not work last week, does he have a job or business?

26

If the answer is yes, the next question is:

5. Why was he absent from work last week?

The interviewer *never* asks whether the person is unemployed or if he or she would like to have a job. Neither the interviewer nor the person interviewed decides whether or not an individual is employed, unemployed, or not in the labor force. This decision, rather, is made automatically by the answers given to the standard questions asked in all interviews. Consequently, criticisms of the validity of the data on employment provided by the survey must be directed not at how the questions are asked but at the questions themselves or, rather, at the concepts of employment and unemployment which underlie them.

Although many legitimate differences of opinion may and do exist on how employment and unemployment should be defined and measured, the most difficult practical problem is to decide whether an individual is looking hard enough for a job as to be really in the labor market. In the household survey the criterion primarily used is activity — what was the person actually doing?

## THE LABOR FORCE

Every person is classified by the household survey as either employed, unemployed, or not in the labor force. The employed and the unemployed together make up the labor force. The basic concepts used are simple. People with jobs are counted as employed. Those persons without jobs who are looking for work are considered unemployed. All other persons are classified as not in the labor force.

Typical cases under the definitions are the following:

• • Jack Smith tells the census interviewer that last week he worked 40 hours as a payroll clerk for the Johnson Soap Company.

• • The wife of Paul Adams reports that her husband lost his job when the Ashtabula Railroad discontinued passenger service. Last week he visited the employment offices of several factories in search of work.

• • Jane Doe is the mother of three boys. Last week she spent all her time at her usual household tasks. Her widowed mother, who lives with the Does, suffers from arthritis and cannot work.

In the examples above, Jack is employed, Paul is unemployed, and Jane and her mother are not in the labor force.

Although most persons can be classified easily in terms of employment status, not everyone fits neatly into a given category. People are considered employed if they did any work at all for pay or profit during the survey week. It does not matter whether this was part-time

27

or temporary work rather than a full-time year-round job. However, persons are also considered as employed, even though they did not work during the survey week, if they had a job they might have been performing. Included in this category as employed are persons absent from work because of illness, vacation, a strike, bad weather, or for personal reasons.

There are other persons, however, who have jobs but nevertheless are counted as unemployed. These are people who are waiting to be called back to a job from which they have been laid off and people who are waiting to report to a new job in 30 days. Before 1957 such individuals were classified as employed, but in that year it was decided to count them as unemployed. This is the only change in definitions which has been made in the labor force series since it started in 1940. It was made because careful study indicated that in too many cases the anticipated recall or new job never materialized and the 30-day waiting period actually represented the beginning of a longer period of unemployment.

There are also persons considered as employed although they receive no pay for their labor. These are people who work 15 hours or more a week in a family owned business. Included in this group would be a boy who works on his father's farm or a wife who helps her husband run a motel.

## Definition of Unemployed

To be counted as unemployed, an individual ordinarily must be without a job and actively seeking employment. Looking for work may consist of such activities as (1) registering at a public or private employment agency, (2) applying directly to employers for work, (3) placing or answering job advertisements, (4) writing letters of application, or (5) waiting for results from any of these activities which were undertaken within the past 60 days.

Some persons are considered as unemployed, even though they are not actively seeking work, because it is felt that under normal circumstances they would be looking for jobs. Examples might be:

• • Jim Stewart has been job hunting for over a month. Last week he was laid up with a leg injury and so did no looking. He will resume his job search, however, as soon as he can get around again.

• • Sam Podbielski lost his job as a welder when the only metalworking plant in his town closed. Although he has looked for three months, he has found no other job he can do. Last week he did not actually look for work, as he felt the effort would be useless.

Another category of unemployed persons has been mentioned previously. These are people who are waiting either to be called back to jobs from which they have been temporarily laid off or are waiting to report to a new job within 30 days.

It is obvious that the dividing lines between the employed, the unemployed, and those not in the labor force are not always distinct and, to a considerable extent, are arbitrary. For example, John Jones, a carpenter, may work for 8 hours for pay during the survey week as a check-out clerk in a grocery store while also looking for a regular job. He is considered employed because he did work for pay. Sara Smith, who usually works as a typist, worked 8 hours as a check-out clerk, but in a store owned by her husband. She too was looking for a regular job. Sara is counted as unemployed because she received no pay and worked less than 15 hours in this family store.

Another situation involves persons who have stopped looking for work because they believe the possibility of finding a job is hopeless. Which persons should be considered unemployed and which not in the labor force? No test of activity can be applied; the only criterion can be how seriously they are interested in wanting a job. The method used to solve this dilemma is to count the person as unemployed only if he *volunteers* the statement that he is not looking for work because he believes no job is available in his occupation or in the community.

This method of ascertaining the degree of an individual's interest in finding work is not satisfactory, since many persons may say that they or members of their families want jobs only because they feel it is expected of them, while other persons who really would like work are less vocal. It seems generally agreed that the census survey underestimates the number of potential job seekers by 800,000 to 1,500,000 persons. That is, these persons are counted as not in the labor force by the survey method but actually would take jobs if they were available.

Despite the difficulties raised by these sorts of problems, it is fair to say that the labor force statistics present an accurate picture of the employment situation. Furthermore, since with the minor exception noted above, the definitions used have not changed, it is a consistent picture over time.

## EMPLOYMENT STATUS OF THE POPULATION

Table 2 provides a summary of the employment status of the working-age population of the United States as measured by the household survey.

*Table 2.* Employment Status of the Non-Institutional Population, January 1965. (Persons 14 years of age and over)

|  | Number | Percent |
|---|---|---|
| Total non-institutional population* | 135,302,000 | 100.0 |
| Total labor force | 75,699,000 | 55.9 |
| Armed forces | 2,707,000 | 2.0 |
| Civilian labor force | 72,992,000 | 53.9 |
| Not in the labor force | 59,603,000 | 44.1 |
| Civilian labor force | 72,992,000 | 100.0 |
| Employed | 68,996,000 | 94.5 |
| At work | 66,634,000 | 91.2 |
| Full time | 53,614,000 | 73.5 |
| Part time | 13,020,000 | 17.8 |
| With a job, but not at work | 2,362,000 | 3.2 |
| Bad weather | 257,000 | 0.4 |
| Industrial dispute | 81,000 | 0.1 |
| Vacation | 345,000 | 0.5 |
| Illness | 1,073,000 | 1.5 |
| Other reasons | 607,000 | 0.8 |
| Unemployed | 3,996,000 | 5.5 |
| Not in the labor force | 59,603,000 | 100.0 |
| Housewives | 35,754,000 | 60.0 |
| Students | 14,328,000 | 24.0 |
| Unable to work | 1,625,000 | 2.7 |
| Other | 7,896,000 | 13.2 |

*Source:* U. S. Bureau of Labor Statistics, *Employment and Earnings,* February 1964, pp. 1, 8, 9.
*Excludes persons in prisons, hospitals, and other custodial institutions.

Examination of Table 2 reveals that the majority of persons 14 years of age and over are in the labor force: they are either working or looking for work. The two major groups not in the labor force are housewives and students. Most of the persons in the labor force are employed and are at work full time (35 hours or more a week). These are constant patterns that exist each month, year in and year out.

Other dimensions of the labor force, however, are not constant but show marked change from month to month. In the summer, for example, the total labor force is swelled by students seeking jobs. In the fall, the totals of the employed and unemployed decline as these youngsters withdraw from the labor force and return to school. In the winter, many construction and other outdoor workers "take it easy" and do not look for jobs, since outside work is not possible. Many persons enter the labor force, on the other hand, in the late autumn or early winter to work in shops and post offices during the Christmas rush.

Thus there is a considerable turnover of persons in the labor force. In 1962, for example, the average size of the civilian labor force was 72 million persons, but 84 million persons were actually in the labor force at some time during the year, working or looking for work. Similarly, while unemployment averaged 4 million persons over the year, over 15 million persons actually experienced unemployment at some time during the year. Indeed, over 5 million persons had two or more spells of unemployment; but only 1.9 million persons looked for work, but found none at all during the year.

Seasonal fluctuations in employment and unemployment are not of particular interest to public officials and others concerned with employment problems. Seasonality of work, however disagreeable to those who would like to work steadily, is normal and largely unavoidable. What we wish to know is whether employment changes from month to month reflect changes in basic economic conditions or only normal seasonal fluctuations. To eliminate the influence of purely seasonal changes on employment figures, a statistical technique called seasonal adjustment is employed. In particular, it is used each month to eliminate the purely seasonal element in the unemployment rate, which has a wide seasonal swing from about 20 percent above the annual average in February to about 20 percent lower than the annual average in October.

It is of interest to compare the seasonally adjusted unemployment rate for January 1965 with the unadjusted rate shown in Table 2 above. The comparison reveals that the seasonally adjusted rate was 4.8 percent, about one-eighth lower than the unadjusted rate of 5.5 percent. This indicates that about a half million of the 3,996,000 unemployed in January 1965 were not working for seasonal reasons—bad weather, slack sales, etc.

The data on insured unemployment under state programs show that 1,996,000 persons were receiving unemployment benefits in January 1965. They amounted to 50 percent of the total unemployed and 4.6 percent of the insured employed.

31

The detailed information on the labor force, including the employed and unemployed, is too extensive for description here. Each month the Department of Labor publishes over 2,000 separate statistics showing employment and unemployment by age, sex, color, marital status, industry, and occupation, with hours of work for the employed and duration of unemployment for the unemployed. From these statistics, hundreds of questions can be answered, such as:

How many of the unemployed were married men?
How many of the unemployed were looking for their first job?
Do Negro women suffer more unemployment than white women?
How many people were employed in manufacturing in Maine?
How many men over 65 were unemployed?

In the next chapter these data will be used to answer the question, "Who are the unemployed?"

# IV

# *Who Are the Unemployed?*

"The major losers in the shifting patterns of manpower supply and demand are the young, the undereducated and unskilled, the laid-off older workers with outmoded skills, and the unemployed caught in communities where the economic base has deteriorated." President Lyndon B. Johnson

THE NATURE of unemployment cannot be expressed in a statistic. The fact that in June 1963, for example, some 4,692,000 persons were jobless only symbolizes the over-all size of the problem. Unemployment happens to individuals, each one of whom is different in background, training, skills, personality, and family responsibilities. Unemployment is the 16-year-old boy, who "dropped out" before completing high school, being told "Company policy requires all employees to have at least a high-school diploma." It is the 35-year-old Negro father of five children able to find only occasional work as a dishwasher. Unemployment is the 47-year-old steel worker, who earned $8,000 in a job now "automated," cashing his last unemployment benefit check and wondering where the grocery money will come from in the future. It is the store owner in a small Montana mining town, bankrupted by the closing of the copper smelter, vainly trying to get a job as a traveling salesman for a hardware firm. Unemployment is these persons, plus millions of other individuals, each needing help suited to his own particular circumstances.

It is, of course, impossible, however desirable it might be, to analyze the individual situation of each person who is out of work, but the unemployed can be divided into meaningful groups on the basis of such characteristics as age, sex, color, family status, occupation, education, etc. Examination of these groupings reveals striking and important differences. In 1963, for example, the total unemployment rate for the country averaged 5.7 percent, but the jobless rate was 2.7 in Iowa and 10.8 in West Virginia. Unemployment amounted to only 1.8 percent for professional and technical workers, but was 12.1 percent for unskilled laborers. Negroes suffered twice as much joblessness as white persons. The unemployment rate for teen-age boys was over 15 percent, that for married men 3.4 percent.

These sizeable differences in the severity of unemployment among various categories of workers suggest that no single remedy is adequate to deal with the problem of joblessness, although three basic programs are generally agreed as necessary vehicles for pushing toward reduction of all kinds of unemployment: (1) an increase of the rate of economic growth, to provide a larger supply of jobs of all kinds; (2) improvement of vocational guidance, employment services, and other devices to aid workers to find jobs; and (3) training and retraining programs to equip people with the skills needed for work. Detailed information about the unemployed is necessary to implement such programs in a practical fashion. Federal spending on building construction is not likely to make jobs for merchant seamen. If construction workers are already fully employed, money spent for new post-office buildings will contribute only to inflation. Vocational guidance programs for high-school dropouts and middle-aged ex-railroad workers must necessarily differ in approach and content. Training programs for women interested in clerical jobs are obviously different from those for men with grade-school educations or less who have spent their lives at unskilled labor.

Knowledge of the characteristics of persons without work is also essential if we are to be able to evaluate the economic and social importance of unemployment. An over-all jobless rate that seems satisfactorily low may conceal serious unemployment in particular sectors of the economy. In 1953, for instance, the rate of unemployment for the labor force as a whole was 2.9 percent, a figure indicating by customary standards a "full-employment" economy. However, the unemployment rate for Negro laborers, the occupational category of about one-quarter of all Negro males, was about 8 percent, denoting for this section of the population a far from satisfactory job situation. Likewise, a large rise in unemployment may not signify as serious a social problem as might be assumed. For example, in June 1964 unemployment rose by 1.1 million persons over the previous month. This increase was due almost entirely to the entrance into the labor market of high school and college students looking for summer jobs or for their first jobs after graduation. It did not mean, therefore, a significant worsening of the employment situation.

34

# MARRIED MEN

The unemployed about whom most concern is felt are married men who are heads of families, with wives and children dependent upon them for support. Fortunately, their rate of unemployment is considerably lower than that for other persons, as shown in the following tabulation:

|  | Unemployment Rate, 1964 |
|---|---|
| Total unemployed | 5.2 |
| *Male* | |
| Married, wife present | 2.8 |
| Single | 11.5 |
| Other marital status* | 8.9 |
| *Female* | |
| Married, husband present | 5.1 |
| Single | 8.7 |
| Other marital status* | 6.4 |

*Widowed, divorced, husband or wife absent.

The lower unemployment rate of married men (it has averaged about 5 percent since 1957, as compared with 8.5 percent for other categories of workers) is due, of course, to the fact that married men tend to be in the prime working years of life, when workers are most likely to have valuable skills, experience, and seniority. Also, married men are not apt to be hunting for their first jobs as are young single people, many of whom are just starting their careers. Unlike married women, who repeatedly leave and re-enter the labor force, married men tend to stick with their jobs.

The unemployment rate of married men fluctuates more sharply with changing economic conditions than do rates for other workers. In good years it may be only half that of women and single men; in depressed years it may rise to three-quarters. Two factors explain this condition. Married men are more concentrated in manufacturing, mining, and other industries which experience large changes in employment and unemployment during business cycles. Also, when layoffs occur, married men seldom leave the labor force, as many women do, but continue searching for work and hence are counted as unemployed.

Since married men who are family heads support three out of every four persons in the United States, any unemployment which they suffer is of serious concern. As noted in the previous discussion, however, married men as a group experience a relatively low rate of unemployment, except when economic conditions are generally depressed.

In the ranks of married men, however, there are individuals who experience frequent or continuing unemployment. This is because they possess characteristics or are in circumstances which seem to be conducive to high rates of joblessness. These characteristics and circumstances affect all sorts of persons regardless of marital status — single men and women, divorced and separated persons, married women, and widows. Basically they involve age, education, occupation, race, and geographic location.

## AGE AND UNEMPLOYMENT

Unemployment is very definitely related to age. Most married men living with their wives are in the 25–64 year male age group, whose members experience the lowest amount of unemployment. The highest rate of unemployment is that of young men and women in their teens. Comparative rates of unemployment by age and sex are shown in Table 3.

The data on unemployment by age reveal a very high rate of unemployment of teen-agers and a comparatively large amount of joblessness among men and women in their early twenties. These high rates

*Table 3.* Unemployed Persons, by Age and Sex, 1963.

| Age and Sex | Thousands of Persons | Unemployment Rate | Percent Unemployed 15 Weeks or Longer |
|---|---|---|---|
| Total | 4,166 | 5.7 | 26.1 |
| Male | 2,537 | 5.3 | 28.2 |
| 14 to 19 years | 566 | 15.5 | 18.7 |
| 20 to 24 years | 396 | 8.8 | 22.2 |
| 25 to 44 years | 830 | 3.7 | 27.8 |
| 45 to 64 years | 647 | 3.9 | 38.0 |
| 65 years and over | 97 | 4.5 | 46.0 |
| Female | 1,629 | 6.5 | 22.9 |
| 14 to 19 years | 413 | 15.7 | 14.8 |
| 20 to 24 years | 262 | 8.9 | 17.9 |
| 25 to 44 years | 573 | 5.9 | 25.0 |
| 45 to 64 years | 351 | 4.0 | 31.6 |
| 65 years and over | 29 | 3.2 | * |

*Source:* Computed from data in *Manpower Report of the President*, March 1964, pp. 200, 203.

*Percent not shown where base is less than 50,000.

cannot be dismissed as being due to high school and college students looking for part-time jobs. The unemployment rate of 14 to 19 year olds not in school actually is double that of students who are in school and also in the labor force. Young people not only have a high unemployment rate, but also make repeated entrances into and exits from the labor force.

Various factors account for the high jobless rate and labor force turnover of young people. Many youngsters swell the ranks of the unemployed during the time they are looking for their first jobs. Others become unemployed as the consequence of leaving jobs which they do not like or for which they are not suited. High school dropouts and some graduates lack any useful skills or training and consequently have difficulty in finding and retaining jobs. The prevalence in industry of the practice of laying off workers in reverse order of seniority results in younger persons being the first to suffer unemployment when business set-backs occur. In addition, the relatively unskilled occupations in which younger workers are largely engaged are especially prone to employment fluctuations. Finally, a significant amount of joblessness among youth results from the failure of job opportunities to increase at a rate adequate to accommodate the expanding numbers of young workers.

The rising unemployment rates for young workers shown in Table 4 indicate an increasingly serious situation for the nation's youth. The inability of the economy since 1957 to provide an adequate supply of jobs has affected new entrants into the job market severely. Furthermore, the net annual increase of the labor force from 1957 to 1962 was

*Table 4.* Unemployment Rates for Workers 16 to 24 Years of Age, 1954–1964.

| Year | Total Civilian Labor Force | Persons 16 to 19 years | Persons 20 to 24 years |
|------|------|------|------|
| 1954 | 5.6 | 11.8 | 8.4 |
| 1955 | 4.4 | 10.3 | 6.3 |
| 1956 | 4.2 | 10.3 | 6.0 |
| 1957 | 4.3 | 11.6 | 7.1 |
| 1958 | 6.8 | 15.9 | 11.2 |
| 1959 | 5.5 | 14.6 | 8.5 |
| 1960 | 5.6 | 14.7 | 8.7 |
| 1961 | 6.7 | 16.8 | 10.4 |
| 1962 | 5.6 | 14.6 | 9.0 |
| 1963 | 5.7 | 17.2 | 8.8 |
| 1964 | 5.2 | 16.2 | 8.3 |

*Source: Manpower Report of the President,* March 1965, p. 198.

37

only 750,000 persons yearly, as compared to 1,100,000 in 1963, 1,259,000 in 1964, and the 1.5 million promised over the next fifteen years. Will the economy be able to do better in placing young people in jobs or will unemployment, with all its attendant problems, continue to grow?

The unemployment rate for men 25 years of age and over is low compared to other groups. These men comprise principally the married men earlier discussed. It will be noted from Table 3, however, that "long-term" unemployment (15 weeks or longer) is directly related to age, both for men and women. That is, while the older worker is less likely to become unemployed than the younger worker, once unemployed he or she has a much more difficult task in finding a new job.

## Women Workers

Unemployment by age shows a pattern for women similar to that for men. The amount of unemployment experienced by adult women is higher than the rate of joblessness for men, a situation resulting primarily from the much looser attachment of women to the labor force. Only half of all employed women work six months or more a year at full-time jobs. The balance work intermittently at full or part-time jobs. This "employment turnover" results in a high rate of reported joblessness. The rate would be even higher were it not for the fact that many women who are without jobs never show up in the unemployment statistics, since they do not look for other work when they leave their jobs and re-enter the labor market only when they have new jobs to move into. Generally, unemployment of women is not regarded as comparable in seriousness to that of men, since a large proportion of women workers (57 percent) are married and living with their husbands or are unmarried teen-agers presumably living at home (9 percent). Only one working woman in ten is head of a family, and about one in four is 20 years old or over and unmarried, widowed, or divorced. This means that only 35 percent of working women, at the most, are the principal breadearners for themselves or a family. In contrast, over three-fourths of men of all ages who are in the labor force are heads of families and presumably their chief financial support. Except for unmarried teen-agers, of course, those men not family heads must ordinarily support themselves.

## Negroes

Data on employment and unemployment need to be differentiated by still another personal characteristic of workers besides sex and age, namely, color. Unemployment rates for non-whites (over 90 percent of whom are Negroes) are twice as high as those for whites. This seems

38

to be due to two main factors. First, because of inadequate education and discrimination in hiring, Negroes are concentrated in the low-skilled occupations subject to heavy unemployment. About half of the difference between the white and non-white unemployment rate seems to be accounted for by occupational distribution. Second, however, there appears to be discrimination against Negroes within occupational groups; in every job group non-white unemployment rates are higher than white rates, as shown in Table 5.

*Table 5.* Unemployment Rates of Experienced Workers,* by Color and Occupation, 1963.

| *Major Occupation Group* | *White* | *Non-White* | *Non-White Rate as Percent of White* |
|---|---|---|---|
| All occupation groups† | 4.4 | 9.3 | 211 |
| Clerical and sales workers | 3.9 | 7.4 | 190 |
| Craftsmen and foremen | 4.6 | 8.2 | 178 |
| Operatives | 6.9 | 11.1 | 161 |
| Private household workers | 3.1 | 7.7 | 248 |
| Other service workers | 5.3 | 10.0 | 187 |
| Farm laborers and foremen | 5.0 | 7.1 | 142 |
| Laborers, except farm and mine | 11.0 | 15.2 | 138 |

*Source: Manpower Report of the President,* March 1964, p. 105.

*The base for the unemployment rate includes the employed, classified according to their current jobs, and the unemployed, classified according to their latest civilian job, if any; it excludes those unemployed persons who never held a full-time civilian job.

†Includes the following groups not shown separately: professional and technical workers; managers, officials and proprietors; farmers and farm managers.

The high amount of joblessness of Negroes working in low-skilled occupations reflects the employment situation of all persons, non-white and white, who have little skill or education. The most important development which is occurring in the labor market is a decreasing demand for unskilled workers and a growing need for well-trained, skilled persons. This transformation in the type of workers needed in the economy results directly from the rapid development of science and technology. New techniques in every field of activity, from medicine to the mining of coal, are requiring more persons with up-to-date skills and fewer persons who can contribute only brawn and muscle to the production process. At the same time advancing technology requires more skilled workers, it is replacing unskilled human labor by machinery.

39

## OCCUPATIONAL TRENDS IN EMPLOYMENT

The changing occupational composition of the nation's work force is reflected in data on employment and unemployment by occupational categories, which are arranged roughly in order of degree of skill levels in Table 6.

*Table 6.* Employed Persons by Occupation, Percentage Distribution, 1900, 1947, 1963, 1975.

| Major Occupational Group | 1900 | Actual 1947 | 1963 | Projected 1975 |
|---|---|---|---|---|
| All groups | 100.0 | 100.0 | 100.0 | 100.0 |
| White-collar workers | 17.6 | 34.9 | 43.9 | 47.8 |
| Professional, technical, and kindred workers | 4.3 | 6.6 | 12.0 | 14.2 |
| Managers, officials, and proprietors, except farm | 5.8 | 10.0 | 10.6 | 10.7 |
| Clerical and kindred workers | 3.0 | 12.4 | 14.9 | 16.2 |
| Sales workers | 4.5 | 5.9 | 6.3 | 6.7 |
| Blue-collar workers | 35.8 | 40.7 | 36.3 | 33.4 |
| Craftsmen, foremen, and kindred workers | 10.5 | 13.4 | 13.0 | 12.8 |
| Operatives and kindred workers | 12.8 | 21.2 | 18.2 | 16.3 |
| Laborers, except farm and mine | 12.5 | 6.1 | 5.2 | 4.3 |
| Service workers | 9.0 | 10.4 | 13.1 | 14.3 |
| Private household workers | 5.4 | 3.0 | 3.4 | — |
| Other service workers | 3.6 | 7.4 | 9.8 | — |
| Farm workers | 37.5 | 14.0 | 6.7 | 4.5 |
| Farmers and farm managers | 19.9 | 8.6 | 3.5 | — |
| Farm laborers and foremen | 17.7 | 5.4 | 3.2 | — |

*Source:* U. S. Bureau of the Census, *Working Paper No. 5,* "Occupational Trends in the United States, 1900 to 1950," p. 7; *Manpower Report of the President,* March 1964, p. 199; *Manpower Report of the President,* March 1963, p. 100.

The data of Table 6 offer several important comparisons: (1) the contrast between the relative importance of major kinds of work at the beginning of the century, when the United States had just become a highly industrialized nation and the movement from farm to city was in full swing, and today; (2) the rapid change in occupations which has taken place in the years since World War II; (3) the further change anticipated over the next decade.

White-collar jobs, most of which require at least a high school education, have been and will continue to grow at a rapid rate. The most

40

skilled occupational group, professional and technical workers, is expanding the fastest of any category. Most workers in professional and technical jobs require advanced training, many of them needing university graduate degrees. Persons in the other white-collar categories possessed in 1964 an average of 12.5 years schooling, indicating that most had a high school education and many had college or other advanced training.

Blue-collar workers, whose ranks expanded in relative importance between the beginning and middle of the century, with the growing industrialization of the country, now are declining in importance as technological advances in manufacturing, mining, transportation, and other fields make it possible to produce more goods and services with fewer workers. The greatest relative decline, it will be noted, is of laborers, whose unskilled work is steadily being replaced by machines — the fork-lift truck, the conveyor line, the power shovel. At the other extreme, skilled craftsmen are holding their own and, indeed are in short supply. Workers in this occupational group would undoubtedly constitute a larger part of the work force than indicated in Table 6 if they were available in the numbers actually needed in industry.

Operatives comprise a wide spread of workers, ranging from railroad brakemen to textile weavers. They are identifiable primarily as persons performing routine tasks requiring a limited amount of training, usually acquired on the job. In contrast, skilled workers perform non-routine work, requiring lengthy formal training. Like unskilled workers, the semiskilled operatives are being displaced by machines.

Service workers, with some exceptions, fill occupations requiring little formal training or skill. They range from hospital attendants to janitors and porters. The proportion of such jobs has been steadily increasing, however, because of the expansion of demand for services and because many of the tasks performed by such workers cannot be done by machines.

The greatest occupational change which has occurred since 1900 has been the decline, both relatively and in absolute numbers, in the persons engaged in agriculture. At the start of the century nearly 11 million persons, over a third of the labor force, worked on farms. Today, only about 5 million persons are so engaged. By 1975, it is estimated, less than 4 million persons (4.5 percent of the labor force) will be working in agriculture. From the standpoint of skills, farming presents a mixed picture. The task of the farmer or farm manager requires more and more skill as the size of individual farms increases and farming techniques advance. The modern farmer must be adept at

a variety of tasks, from livestock management to equipment maintenance and bookkeeping. In contrast to the high skill required of the
farm operator, however, the farm hand has usually been an unskilled
worker. Indeed, agriculture has been a major source of employment
for dropouts from school and others deficient in formal education or
training. In 1964, farm laborers averaged only 8.5 years of schooling,
the lowest amount of any occupational group. Disappearance of farm
jobs is contributing heavily to the high rate of unemployment of the
poorly educated and unskilled.

## EDUCATION AND UNEMPLOYMENT

The impact of changing skill requirements on employment is also
reflected in Table 7, which shows the percentage of experienced workers
in each occupational category unemployed in 1963. If it were possible
to include in the table the number of jobless youths without previous
work experience, a large proportion of whom in the past have found
their first employment in low-skilled jobs, the unemployment ratios for
unskilled or low-skilled occupations would be even higher. Table 7
indicates clearly the relationship of unemployment and skill. In the

*Table 7.* Unemployed as a Percentage of Experienced Workers in
Major Occupational Groups, 1963.

| Major Occupational Group | Unemployment Rate, 1963 |
|---|---|
| White-collar workers | 2.8 |
| Professional, technical and kindred workers | 1.8 |
| Managers, officials, and proprietors, except farm | 1.5 |
| Clerical and kindred workers | 4.0 |
| Sales workers | 4.2 |
| Blue-collar workers | 7.2 |
| Craftsmen, foremen and kindred workers | 4.8 |
| Operatives and kindred workers | 7.4 |
| Laborers, except farm and mine | 12.1 |
| Service workers | 6.0 |
| Private household workers | 5.2 |
| Other service workers | 6.2 |
| Farm workers | 3.0 |
| Farmers and farm managers | .5 |
| Farm laborers and foremen | 5.5 |

*Source:* U. S. Bureau of Labor Statistics, *Employment and Earnings,* February
1964, p. 76.

white-collar occupations, professional workers and managers, whose work is highly skilled, have a much lower unemployment rate than clerks and salesmen, most of whom perform relatively simple tasks. The increase in unemployment as skill level drops is also very well-defined in the blue-collar group. The contrast between farm managers and laborers has already been discussed.

Job skill and amount of education are closely related. The data in Table 8, showing that unemployment is inversely related to level of education, therefore should produce no surprise, since they simply confirm that skilled persons are in far greater demand in the labor market than are the unskilled. What is particularly significant in Table 8 is the increase in rates of unemployment between 1950 and 1962 of those who did not complete high school. In contrast, the very low unemployment rate for college graduates fell by more than a third between 1950 and 1962.

Proponents of the theory that unemployment is mainly due to

*Table 8.* Unemployment in Relation to Education, Males, 18 Years and Over, 1950 to 1962.

| Years of School Completed | Unemployment Rates | | | | | Percentage Change in Rate 1950 to 1962 |
| | April 1950 | Oct. 1952 | March 1957 | March 1959 | March 1962 | |
| --- | --- | --- | --- | --- | --- | --- |
| Elementary: 0 to 4 years | 8.6 | 2.1 | 8.0 | 9.9 | 10.4 | +20.9 |
| 5 to 7 years | 8.3 | 2.4 | 6.2 | 9.7 | 8.5 | + 2.4 |
| 8 years | 6.6 | 1.4 | 4.4 | 7.3 | 7.5 | +13.6 |
| High school: 0 to 3 years | 6.9 | 1.6 | 4.7 | 8.1 | 7.8 | +13.0 |
| 4 years | 4.6 | 1.1 | 3.0 | 4.9 | 4.8 | + 4.3 |
| College: 1 to 3 years | 4.1 | 1.1 | 2.7 | 3.3 | 4.0 | − 2.4 |
| 4 years or more | 2.2 | 0.4 | 0.6 | 1.4 | 1.4 | −36.4 |
| All groups | 6.2 | 1.5 | 4.1 | 6.3 | 6.0 | − 3.2 |

*Source:* Charles C. Killingsworth, testimony before Subcommittee on Employment and Manpower, Committee on Labor and Public Welfare, U. S. Senate, *Nation's Manpower Revolution*, Part 5, pp. 1476–1482 (1963); U. S. Bureau of the Census, *Current Population Reports: Labor Force*, "Educational Attainment and Literacy of Workers: October 1952," Series P-50, No. 49 (October 1953), p. 7; U. S. Bureau of the Census, *Current Population Reports: Labor Force*, "Educational Attainment of Workers: March 1954," Series P-50, No. 78 (November 1957), p. 7; U. S. Bureau of Labor Statistics, "Special Labor Force Report No. 1: Educational Attainment of Workers, 1959," by Arnold Katz, *Monthly Labor Review*, February 1960, Reprint No. 2333, p. A-6; U. S. Bureau of Labor Statistics, "Special Labor Force Report No. 30: Educational Attainment of Workers, March 1962," by Denis F. Johnston, *Monthly Labor Review*, May 1963, Reprint No. 2416, p. A-6.

structural changes in the economy point to the variation in unemployment with amount of education as support for their view. They further argue that unemployment rates in themselves do not indicate the full extent of the shift in job opportunities brought about by the increasing demand for skilled workers. Substantial numbers of the poorly educated, it is asserted, having given up the effort to find jobs, have withdrawn from the labor force. Table 9 shows changes in labor force participation rates by years of school completed between 1950 and 1962. These rates, it should be noted, are for males, 18 years of age and over, a group traditionally considered as active workers. At the lowest level of educational attainment, 0–4 years of school, only three out of four men were working or looking for work in 1950; by 1962, the proportion had fallen to three out of five. Labor force participation rates for all men without high school training have fallen sharply. Perhaps the most startling revelation is that only among men with some education beyond high school has there been an increase in labor force participation.

*Table 9.* Labor Force Participation Rates by Years of School, Males, 18 Years and Over, 1950 to 1962.

| Years of School Completed | Labor Force Participation Rates | | | | | Percentage |
|---|---|---|---|---|---|---|
| | April 1950 | Oct. 1952 | March 1957 | March 1959 | March 1962 | Change in Rate 1950 to 1962 |
| Elementary: 0 to 4 years | 74.6 | 73.3 | 65.2 | 63.5 | 58.3 | −21.9 |
| 5 to 7 years | 85.0 | 82.3 | 81.7 | 77.7 | 74.6 | −12.2 |
| 8 years | 88.1 | 87.7 | 83.8 | 82.6 | 78.2 | −11.2 |
| High school: 1 to 3 years | 92.1 | 91.6 | 90.7 | 90.0 | 88.8 | − 3.6 |
| 4 years | 94.0 | 93.1 | 93.6 | 92.7 | 90.7 | − 3.5 |
| College: 1 to 3 years | 79.6 | 85.6 | 83.2 | 83.4 | 83.0 | + 4.3 |
| 4 or more years | 92.1 | 88.0 | 92.3 | 92.8 | 92.3 | + 0.2 |
| All groups | 87.6 | 87.3 | 86.0 | 85.2 | 83.5 | − 4.7 |

*Source:* Same as Table 8.

## EMPLOYMENT BY INDUSTRY

Partly reflected in the data on employment by occupation discussed above has been a significant shift in the distribution of employment by industry, resulting mainly from the same technological advance that has caused a redistribution of workers among occupations. Data on employment by industries is presented in Table 10.

44

The decline in agricultural employment, a consequence of advance in agricultural science and techniques, has already been discussed.

*Table 10.* Employment in Industry Divisions, 1947–1975.*

| Industry Division | 1947 | Actual 1956 | 1963 | Projected 1975 |
|---|---|---|---|---|
| | Employment in Thousands | | | |
| Goods-producing industries | 26,738 | 27,636 | 25,644 | 29,300 |
| Agriculture | 8,256 | 6,572 | 4,946 | 3,900 |
| Mining | 955 | 822 | 634 | 700 |
| Construction | 1,982 | 2,999 | 3,029 | 4,400 |
| Manufacturing | 15,545 | 17,243 | 17,035 | 20,300 |
| Service-producing industries | 25,399 | 31,344 | 36,476 | 48,700 |
| Transportation and public utilities | 4,166 | 4,244 | 3,913 | 4,500 |
| Trade | 8,955 | 10,858 | 11,865 | 15,600 |
| Finance, insurance, and real estate | 1,754 | 2,429 | 2,866 | 3,900 |
| Services and miscellaneous | 5,050 | 6,536 | 8,297 | 11,900 |
| Government | 5,474 | 7,277 | 9,535 | 12,800 |
| Federal | 1,892 | 2,209 | 2,358 | — |
| State and local | 3,582 | 5,069 | 7,177 | — |
| Total employment | 52,137 | 58,980 | 62,120 | 78,000 |
| | Percentage Distribution | | | |
| Goods-producing industries | 51.2 | 46.9 | 41.3 | 37.5 |
| Agriculture | 15.8 | 11.1 | 8.0 | 5.0 |
| Mining | 1.8 | 1.4 | 1.0 | 0.9 |
| Construction | 3.8 | 5.0 | 4.9 | 5.6 |
| Manufacturing | 29.8 | 29.2 | 27.4 | 26.0 |
| Service-producing industries | 48.8 | 53.1 | 58.7 | 62.5 |
| Transportation and public utilities | 8.0 | 7.2 | 6.3 | 5.8 |
| Trade | 17.2 | 18.4 | 19.1 | 20.0 |
| Finance, insurance, and real estate | 3.4 | 4.1 | 4.6 | 5.0 |
| Services and miscellaneous | 9.7 | 11.1 | 13.4 | 15.3 |
| Government | 10.5 | 12.3 | 15.3 | 16.4 |
| Federal | 3.6 | 3.7 | 3.8 | — |
| State and local | 6.9 | 8.6 | 11.5 | — |
| Total employment | 100.0 | 100.0 | 100.0 | 100.0 |

*Source:* Computed from data in *Manpower Report of the President,* March 1964, pp. 195, 226, 244.

*Data for agriculture include self-employed and unpaid family workers. Data for other industries exclude these categories and represent only employees receiving wages or salaries. Omission of self-employed workers (6,195,000 in 1963) and unpaid family workers (587,000 in 1963) distorts somewhat the distribution of persons among industries, since the self-employed and unpaid family workers are mainly found in trade, services, and finance, insurance, and real estate.

A steady decline likewise has been occurring in mining, again the result of new techniques and increasing mechanization. Also contributing importantly to the decline of mining employment have been the inroads made into markets for coal by other fuels, such as petroleum and natural gas. Employment in bituminous coal mining, for example, dropped from 426,000 in 1947 to 137,000 in 1963, a fall of two-thirds in only 16 years.

Employment in manufacturing industries grew until 1956. Since then, it has remained relatively constant and seems destined to increase by only a modest amount between now and 1975. Even this increase may not occur if new labor-saving techniques are introduced on a large scale. Workers engaged directly in production have declined in numbers since 1956; non-production workers on the other hand — that is managers, engineers, technicians, clerks, etc. — have been steadily increasing in numbers. In 1963 they constituted over 26 percent of all manufacturing employees, as compared to only 16 percent at the end of World War II.

Only construction, among the goods-producing industries, seems destined to experience a large increase in jobs over the next decade.

Prior to 1956, the majority of Americans were engaged in the production of goods. Since 1956, the service-producing industries, with the exception of transportation and public utilities, have been expanding at a rapid rate and now employ the majority of workers. The reasons lie in expanded consumer demand for all kinds of services and our inability to substitute machines for manpower in many of these industries. In the one service sector where machines are extensively used, transportation and public utilities, it is notable that employment is decreasing.

Increasing job opportunities in the service-producing industries do not necessarily provide employment for workers displaced from goods-producing industries. The two kinds of industries may use different kinds of workers in terms of sex, age, training, and skills. Service industries also have greater need of low-wage, part-time employees than do goods-producing industries. Thus a 40-year-old male electrotype caster permanently displaced from his job in the printing business by a new reproduction process can't qualify, for example, as a dental hygienist, one of the rapidly growing service jobs employing women. Nor can the coal miner rendered jobless by new machines find work in the rapidly expanding occupation of credit manager. A 30-year-old textile weaver with a family to support does not want to take part-time employment as a drug store clerk.

# DEPRESSED AREAS

The changing industrial pattern in the United States has also created serious job problems geographically. The decline of employment in various industries has caused large-scale joblessness in the areas where these industries have been located. Anthracite coal mining, for example, is concentrated in a small area of Pennsylvania, of which Wilkes-Barre and Scranton are the principal cities. With the displacement of anthracite for home heating by fuel oil and natural gas, output of hard coal has declined from an average of 60 million tons a year during World War II to about 18 million tons at present. Employment has fallen from 90,000 workers in 1940 to 10,000 workers today. As a result, unemployment rates in the Scranton and Wilkes-Barre areas have ranged from 8.6 to 24.2 percent during the past eight years. Such new industry as has developed in these areas has not offered the kind of work for which ex-miners can qualify.

Labor shortages may exist, on the other hand, in areas where industries are developing. Mobile as the American population seems to be, it is not an easy matter for unemployed persons to move from one area to another in search of work. Only 25 percent of a group of unemployed persons interviewed in April 1962 indicated they would accept a job in another part of the country. Most persons would not accept a job elsewhere because of family and home ties in their present community.

Other factors also contribute to unemployment in particular localities, including the shifting of consumer markets away from the area, major firms in the area going out of business for various reasons, depletion of natural resources such as timber or ore, etc.

The consequence of all these factors is the appearance of "distressed areas" — communities or regions with very high rates of unemployment as compared to other areas. In 1963, as an illustration, the national unemployment rate was 5.7 percent, but rates for individual localities among the 150 major labor market areas in the United States ranged from a low of 2.4 percent in Washington, D. C. to a high of 14.5 percent in Johnstown, Pennsylvania.

Unemployment in distressed areas has a severe impact on the people involved, because it lasts so long a time. Moreover, it may require the unemployed to make a painful major readjustment in order to find work — changing to a new occupation or moving to a new location.

In rural areas, unemployment may not show up directly as so many men and women totally out of work, since there is always work to do on a farm which may be sufficient to keep a person from being considered "unemployed." In actual fact, however, the economic value of the individual's activity may be so low that he should be considered, if not

47

DOCUMENTS
Kansas City, Mo.

unemployed, "underemployed." It is estimated that underemployment in agriculture currently amounts to a million persons. Unemployment in rural areas also is "less visible" because a high proportion of farm youths, recognizing their limited job opportunities at home, migrate to urban areas in search of work.

## The Unemployed Individual

As an answer to the question "Who are the unemployed?" relating joblessness to such factors as age, education, race, sex, or occupation is only a partially satisfactory solution. Individual men and women confront the job market at various ages, with differing amounts of education, work experience, occupational skills, and other characteristics. No person can be categorized by age alone or by any other single factor, be it race, occupation, or locality in which he or she lives. Each individual possesses a variety of characteristics which affect his or her employment experience in different ways.

Most persons, fortunately, possess a combination of "employment characteristics" in which the positive factors are dominant so that they experience little, if any, unemployment. For example, a middle-aged man possesses only an eighth-grade education and lives in a depressed area, but his years of work experience in an essential job make him invaluable to his firm, which is in a growth industry. Or a 19-year-old girl is able to find work, despite a scarcity of jobs for young people, because she has been trained as a dental hygienist, an occupation where workers are in very short supply. The majority of people have one or more negative employment characteristics working against them — age, sex, lack of education, a job in a declining industry, and the like — but happily are aided by positive characteristics which make them desirable employees.

The unfortunate persons with work histories marked by frequent, and often lengthy, periods of unemployment are the individuals whose employment characteristics are predominantly negative. A tragic example is provided by Negro teen-agers, 30 percent of whom were unemployed during 1963, as compared to 14 percent of white teen-agers and 5.7 percent of the labor force as a whole. This 30 percent is a national average for both sexes. For example, for Negro girls with markedly inferior educations, living in cities with high jobless levels, the unemployment rate may average 50 percent. Negroes suffer from various negative employment characteristics. Many have had inferior educations and are unable to enter apprenticeship and other vocational training programs. Racial prejudice denies them jobs, and the job protection afforded by union membership is enjoyed by relatively few

Negroes. As the consequence, Negroes have access mainly to the low-skilled jobs characterized by frequent layoffs or part-time work. Over the long run, furthermore, these unskilled manual jobs are decreasing in number.

Of the various employment characteristics discussed in this chapter, the amount and quality of education which an individual has received are unquestionably the most important. This is borne out in many ways. A direct relation between years of school completed and unemployment was shown in Table 8. A comparison of high school graduates in 1962 with young people who "dropped out" of school in the same year revealed a 14 percent rate of unemployment for the graduates, versus a 29 percent rate for the dropouts. Higher in the age scale, the same picture has been revealed by studies of the unemployed. One such investigation found that 60 percent of a group of hard-core unemployed, 35 to 50 years old, had not completed high school. Many were actually illiterate.

A dramatic example of the influence of education on employment has been provided by Secretary of Labor W. Willard Wirtz. Census figures for 1960 showed an unemployment rate of 35.5 percent in one neighborhood in Chicago, whose population was 97 percent Negro. In another neighborhood, whose population was 96 percent Negro, the unemployment rate was 2.1 percent. In the first neighborhood, years of school completed averaged only 8.5; in the second neighborhood, the average was 12.2.

As more and more young people enter a labor market demanding ever higher levels of training and skill, education will play an increasingly important role. To quote Secretary Wirtz, "A boy or girl who drops out of school today without an elemental skill comes awfully close to committing economic suicide; for the number of unskilled jobs is getting smaller and smaller each year."

49

# V

# *What Causes Unemployment?*

> "Since a man may be jobless for a number of different reasons, classifications of unemployment by causes would — if it were possible to quantify them — add up to well over 100 percent of the unemployed." Joint Economic Committee, *Unemployment: Terminology, Measurement, and Analysis.*

UNEMPLOYMENT is often thought of as an "economic disease," that is, as a malfunctioning of the economic system, which should provide jobs for all would-be workers if it is in a "healthy" condition. The analogy is, from several aspects, a good one. In view of the unmet needs of the nation — for example, those of the nearly one-fifth of American families who live in poverty — a properly functioning economy should be using all of its productive resources, including labor, just as a soundly functioning organism uses all of its members. From another aspect, the suffering and personal and social deterioration which accompany unemployment may be compared to the pain and debilitation associated with illness. Diagnosis of the causes of unemployment, as with those of a physical ailment, is essential to achieving a lasting cure, but such diagnosis is frequently difficult and beset by "complications." Finally, it might be observed that "treatment" of unemployment frequently involves measures which reduce symptoms but do not get at causes and that some "patients" (that is, the "short-term" unemployed) are easily restored to full activity, while others (the "hard-core" unemployed) may be beyond effective help.

In their efforts to determine the causes of unemployment so that remedies may be prescribed, economists classify joblessness into various types: seasonal, cyclical, technological, frictional, structural, irregular, personal, normal, chronic, and so on. Altogether, it is estimated, some

70 terms and classifications have appeared in publications on the subject. This plethora of names has come about because classification has been used as a tool for the understanding of some particular aspect of unemployment or for the presentation of a particular point of view. Some classifications simply reflect statistical methods by which data on joblessness have been collected and analyzed. In any event, the potpourri of adjectives affixed to the term unemployment has probably contributed as much confusion as enlightenment to understanding of the problem.

Certain classifications of unemployment, however, enjoy widespread acceptance and are highly useful, provided one bears constantly in mind that these "kinds" of unemployment usually do not exist in pure form but are intermixed and interdependent in real life. As with names of physical illnesses, these terms serve to identify characteristics and possible causes of various manifestations of the disease of unemployment.

## Seasonal Unemployment

"Seasonal" unemployment is the term used to describe changes in employment which occur regularly each year and result from climatic or weather changes or temporary but recurrent demand factors such as holiday buying and annual model changes. Examples may be found in construction, where winter weather limits outside work; in children's toy departments, where most sales occur in the Christmas season; in automobile manufacturing, where production ceases for several weeks in the summer to permit changing tools and dies for the new models. On the supply side of the labor market, an influx of students seeking temporary work swells the ranks of the unemployed each summer. Employment is subject to such a great degree of seasonality, month to month, that as was noted in Chapter III, government data on employment and unemployment are "seasonally adjusted" to eliminate ups and downs due purely to seasonal factors.

## Frictional Unemployment

"Frictional" unemployment results from the fact that in a large, complex, and changing economy there is not a perfect or immediate matching of unemployed people and vacant jobs. Persons lose or quit jobs and cannot immediately locate new ones. Job openings may not be discovered because they are not advertised or, more likely, the unemployed person conducts his search for work in a haphazard and inefficient manner. Available jobs may be situated some distance away from where job seekers live. Work which is currently being offered may not be suitable for the persons presently in the job market. New workers, entering the labor market for the first time, also encounter these difficulties and in addition may change jobs several times before finding suitable employment.

## Normal Unemployment

It is fairly common for the term frictional unemployment to be used as a catch-all phrase embracing all short-term unemployment, including seasonal unemployment. Frequently, such use carries the implication that this is a minimum or irreducible level of unemployment characteristic of an economic system in which employers are free to vary the size of their work forces and workers are free to change jobs. Perhaps most economists, however, would argue that the term "frictional" should be restricted to unemployment arising from the imperfection of the job market. "Normal" unemployment is suggested as a better term for use as a catch-all to embrace frictional, seasonal, irregular, personal, and related types of short-term unemployment.

## Structural Unemployment

"Structural" unemployment is one of the types most difficult to define clearly and consistently. The distinction between "frictional" and "structural" unemployment is not sharp; the two classifications easily blend into each other. Both result from difficulties in adjusting the supply of workers to the demand for them in a dynamic economic system in which there are continuous changes in technology, in consumer tastes, in plant location, and in the composition, distribution, and uses of labor and other resources. Frictional unemployment is best used to describe short-run joblessness resulting from the individual's difficulty in locating and moving into an available job. Structural unemployment, on the other hand, implies joblessness resulting from major long-run changes in the composition of the labor force and in the industrial, occupational, and geographical location of job opportunities.

A good illustration of structural unemployment is provided by the job losses suffered by West Virginia coal miners. Here several kinds of structural factors have caused unemployment: (1) mechanization of mining operations, (2) a switch by fuel users from coal to oil and gas, (3) the non-transferability of miners' skills to other types of work, and (4) the failure of West Virginia to attract the new and expanding industries of the nation, most of which have found locations far removed from the Appalachian region.

"Technological" unemployment is a term widely used to identify a particular type of structural unemployment — the displacement of workers by new machines or new methods of production. To the extent that automation puts workers out of jobs, it is causing "technological" unemployment. As a means of identifying a cause of unemployment, this term is useful. There is some risk, however, of overemphasis of the role of new methods and machines in causing unemployment when actually it is other kinds of structural shifts which are chiefly responsible.

## IRREGULAR AND PERSONAL UNEMPLOYMENT

"Irregular" unemployment is used to describe job losses resulting from unusual developments such as strikes, floods, fires, material shortages, etc.

"Personal" or "personal problem" unemployment, often referred to as "unemployability," includes job-seekers who have difficulty finding work because of personal characteristics or deficiencies. This would include perhaps three chief groups: (1) those who have mental or physical handicaps or personality problems which prevent their being productive workers; (2) those with limited education or training, persons difficult to train for new jobs, etc.; (3) those whose availability to work is limited because of their own personal decisions as to nature, time, and location of work.

## CYCLICAL UNEMPLOYMENT

The types of unemployment so far discussed are mainly attributable to the inability of job seekers to locate, move to, or qualify for the jobs which are available in various parts of the economy. Unemployment may also result, however, from another cause — the failure of the economy to provide a sufficient number of jobs. Two classifications of unemployment resulting from inadequate demand for labor are generally recognized.

"Cyclical" unemployment is the term used to describe the cutback in employment which occurs during the recession phase of the business cycle. Its severity is related to the degree of decline in sales and business activity. In July 1957, when the business cycle was at a peak of prosperity, unemployment totaled only 2,845,000 persons; thereafter business activity turned down, and at the bottom of the resulting recession joblessness totalled over 5,000,000 persons in April 1958.

Until recently, most persons have tended to think of business depression as the major cause of unemployment, and most efforts to combat unemployment have been directed toward the goal of eliminating cyclical fluctuations in business activity. The thought has been that if economic operations were maintained at a "prosperity" level, only an irreducible minimum of "normal" unemployment would exist.

The steady growth of unemployment over the past decade has cast doubt, however, on the notion that the business cycle alone is responsible for most unemployment. Each business cycle peak since 1953 has been accompanied by a larger amount of unemployment. From 2.5 percent of the labor force in 1953, unemployment rose to 4.3 percent in 1957, 5.6 percent in 1960, and 5.7 percent in 1963. This phenomenon has led to suggestions of yet another classification of unemployment.

## GROWTH-GAP UNEMPLOYMENT

The newest type of unemployment to be recognized, one for which no name has yet been agreed on, is thought to result from an inadequate rate of growth of the economy. For this reason, the term "growth-gap" unemployment has been suggested. Various factors, such as high tax rates, unbalanced distribution of personal income, and monopolistic restraints of trade, it is argued, prevent consumer spending and business investment from increasing rapidly enough to provide the continuous creation of new jobs needed to match (a) the increase in size of the labor force resulting from population growth and the rising proportion of the population seeking employment, and (b) the elimination of jobs by technological advances which reduce the number of workers needed to produce a given output of goods and services.

Those who argue that inadequate economic growth is responsible for the current high level of unemployment advocate measures to increase consumer spending and business investment. Principal emphasis has been placed upon reduction of federal, personal, and corporate income tax rates, an action carried out by the Congress in 1964.*

## PART-TIME UNEMPLOYMENT

The types or classifications of unemployment so far discussed have been concerned with causes of joblessness. Unemployment also may be classified in another way — by the manner in which it discloses or disguises itself. Ordinarily, we think of an unemployed man or woman as being clearly identifiable: he or she does not have a job and wants one. A considerable amount of unemployment, however, does not show up, at least in statistics or by casual observation, in such an obvious manner. In the language of economists, it exists as "disguised" unemployment.

---

*This tax reduction added about $9 billion to consumer expenditures in 1964. The unemployment rate fell from 5.0% in the first part of the year to 4.5% in the last three months.

One form of disguised unemployment is part-time work performed by persons who would prefer to work full time. In 1964, over 15 million persons (about one-fifth of those at work) were employed, on the average, less than 35 hours per week. More than half of these persons, largely students and housewives, preferred part-time work; 30 percent of the group, persons who normally work full time, put in short work weeks for various non-economic reasons, such as bad weather, brief illnesses, strikes, holidays, etc. The remaining sixth of the part-time workers, some 2.5 million persons, were divided into two roughly equal groups: (a) regular full-time workers whose hours were cut because of slack work, shortages of materials, repairs to plant and equipment, or because they ended or began a job during the week; and (b) workers who worked part time because they could only find a part-time job or a series of jobs which added up to less than a full work week.

The number of persons who work part time and the proportion which they constitute of the work force has risen greatly in the past fifteen years. About four of every ten additional workers employed in the United States since 1950 have taken part-time jobs by choice. The most important factor accounting for the rise in persons looking for part-time work has been the increase in labor force participation by women, who accounted for nearly three-fifths of the entire increase in the nation's work force between 1947 and 1964. Mainly because of family responsibilities, about one-fifth of employed women work part time for non-economic reasons, as contrasted to only 6 percent of men. Other factors contributing to the increase in part-time workers have been rising school attendance, which has reduced full-time work among youth 14 to 24 years of age, and the earlier retirement of older people, many of whom, while withdrawing from full-time work, seek part-time jobs to supplement their pensions or other income.

At the same time that the numbers of persons seeking part-time work have grown, the availability of part-time employment has increased, as the result of the expansion of retail trade and services. Part-time employment in such industries as mining, manufacturing, and construction results nearly entirely from economic factors — slack business, seasonality, etc. Only 3 percent of manufacturing employees work fewer than 35 hours a week by preference, as compared to about one in five workers in trade and services.

To some extent, the growth of part-time jobs has been a cause of unemployment for men, since many such jobs, while suited to female skills and needs, are not compatible with the abilities and income requirements of male workers.

The amount of part time worked by regular full-time workers is primarily a function of the business cycle. When business activity slumps, hours of work are reduced, especially in manufacturing, mining, and construction. As business recovers, hours are increased.

The number of workers who usually work part time because they cannot find the full-time jobs they would like to have has increased by nearly 60 percent since 1950. In 1964, such persons, who numbered 1.3 million and constituted 8.5 percent of all part-time workers, averaged only 17.6 hours of work a week. The proportion of non-white men and women working short work weeks for economic reasons is three times the proportion of white persons.

Only about 15 percent of the unemployed seek part-time jobs. Three-fourths of these are teen-agers, men over 65, and women aged 45–65 years. Only 2 percent are men in the 20–65 year-old group.

Concern over the counterpart of part-time work, which might be called "part-time unemployment," has caused the United States Department of Labor to publish a special unemployment rate, labeled "labor force time lost through unemployment and part-time work." It expresses the man-hours lost by the unemployed and those on part time for economic reasons as a percent of the man-hours which might be worked if all members of the labor force worked full time, which is defined as 35 hours or more per week. In April 1964, on a seasonally adjusted basis, 4,024,000 persons were totally unemployed. This amounted to 5.4 percent of the civilian labor force. In addition, however, 2,146,000 persons worked only part time "for economic reasons" — that is, the full-time work they desired was not available. Adding the hours not worked by these part-time workers to the hours not worked by those totally unemployed produced an unemployment rate of 5.9 percent. In other words, part-time unemployment amounted to 0.5 percent of potential work time. This, furthermore, represents a conservative estimate; although an individual working 35 hours a week is considered in the official statistics to be employed full time, hours worked by all employed persons in April 1964 averaged 40.0.

About 32 percent, or one-third, of all employed persons work over 40 hours per week on the average. For many of these individuals, such as physicians, college teachers, proprietors of stores and service establishments, or farmers, long hours of work are normal. For other persons, however, such as employees of manufacturing concerns, work in excess of 40 hours a week constitutes overtime. Recently, unions have protested strongly against such overtime work, arguing that if employers would hire additional workers, instead of using present employees on an overtime basis, unemployment could be reduced.

## "Not in the Labor Force"

Another type of disguised unemployment, to which reference was made earlier, involves those persons who do not try to search for work because they believe there is no chance of finding a job. In the employment statistics these individuals are classified as not in the labor force, rather than as unemployed. Estimates of their number currently range from 800,000 to 1,500,000. An indication that this type of disguised unemployment is a form of structural unemployment is provided by examination of the classes of persons who have been withdrawing from the labor force.

The labor force participation rate of young persons, 14 to 24 years of age, has dropped considerably in recent years, as unemployment rates in this age group have mounted. In 1963 over a third of a million young men under the age of 25 were neither in school nor in the labor force; they were not trying to obtain jobs and so were not included in the labor force. At the other end of the age ladder, men 65 and older have withdrawn from the labor force in large numbers. In 1947 about 48 percent of men 65 and over were employed or looking for work; in 1963 only 28 percent were so engaged.

Negro men, who suffer twice the rate of unemployment of white men, at the same time have a lower rate of labor force participation. There is no question but that this reflects the Negro's despair over finding work and his abandonment of the effort, for few Negro families have income other than that received from work. This is confirmed by the markedly higher rate of participation in the labor force of Negro women than white women.

Underlying the withdrawal from the labor force of young, old, and Negro men is a common factor, the decrease in job opportunities for the poorly educated. Technological advance has replaced unskilled labor by machines, while the new employment opportunities which have appeared require ever higher levels of education. Thus, young persons who previously could find an ample number of jobs requiring no training or preparation are now remaining in school in order to acquire the education needed in today's world. Older men, on the other hand, find it difficult to obtain the training which they need and impossible to obtain jobs without it. Inadequate education is, of course, one of the chief handicaps suffered by Negroes and an important part of the reason for their high rate of unemployment. The role of lack of education in causing disguised unemployment was pointed up in Table 9, which shows that only among men who have attended college has there not been a drop in labor force participation in recent years.

57

## UNDEREMPLOYMENT

Hidden unemployment takes yet another disguise: persons working in jobs in which their output is very low. The principal location of this form of disguised unemployment is in agriculture. It is estimated that about one million persons engaged in farming are superfluous; that is, that their withdrawal from agriculture would cause an insignificant drop in the output of farm products. These individuals primarily are members of families living on small, unimproved farms which yield little more than bare subsistence. Other persons whose productive efforts yield little income are scattered through the economy. Chiefly, they are owners of small business establishments or individuals engaged in menial service occupations.

## LONG-TERM UNEMPLOYMENT

In the course of an average year, quite a large number of persons experience unemployment. The answer to the question, "do all of these persons suffer severe hardship," is obviously no. Being without work for a few days or even a few weeks is frustrating and inconvenient, but normally does not create serious personal or social problems. However, unemployment continuing for many weeks, months, or even years produces overwhelming difficulties for the jobless worker and his dependents. Few families have the savings or other resources to finance an extended period without income. Two in every five individuals are not eligible for unemployment insurance benefits and these when received average only 35 percent of regular earnings. Extended unemployment thus means piling up bills, cutting down purchases, getting help from relatives, moving to cheaper housing — eventually, perhaps, becoming a recipient of public welfare.

What is the dividing line between short-term and long-term unemployment? Any boundary, it should be obvious, must be arbitrary, for no distinction can be made that is suitable for all purposes or applicable to every situation. The United States Department of Labor uses 15 weeks as the dividing point between short- and long-term joblessness. In its reports on the long-term unemployed, the Labor Department usually presents detailed information on the characteristics of those unemployed 15 weeks and over and those unemployed 27 weeks and over. In popular discussion, members of the latter group are often referred to as the "hard-core" unemployed.

The average duration of unemployment is closely related to the business cycle, indicating that long-term joblessness is an aspect of cyclical unemployment. In 1948, for example, a year of prosperity, the average unemployed person was out of work a little over 8½ weeks, but in 1950, partially a year of recession, the average duration of unemployment was over 12 weeks. By 1953, it had fallen again to just over 8 weeks.

Since the end of the Korean War, however, there has been an alarming uptrend in the length of unemployment. Persons unemployed 15 weeks or more averaged 16 percent of the total unemployed between 1947 and 1953; from 1954 through 1964, they averaged over 25 percent.

The proportion of persons suffering long-term unemployment is higher for non-whites than for whites, for men than for women, for blue-collar workers than for white-collar workers, for older than for younger workers. Although younger workers are subject to more frequent spells of unemployment, the older a person is, the more likely it is he will remain unemployed when he does lose his job.

The number of persons experiencing unemployment during the course of a year is considerably higher than the average number of persons unemployed during the year. Because most of the unemployed are jobless for only a few weeks at a time, there is a large "turnover" in the ranks of the unemployed. In 1963, for example, monthly unemployment averaged 3,876,000, but some 14,211,000 individuals were jobless for varying periods of time during the year. The 14.2 million individuals who were unemployed in 1963 constituted 16.7 percent, or about one in six, of the total of 85 million persons who worked or looked for work during the year. While 1963 was a year of high unemployment, even in years when the average rate of unemployment is low, 13 percent or more of those in the labor force during the year experience unemployment.

The effects of unemployment on income and living standards are closely related to the frequency and length of joblessness. Only for a small portion of those experiencing unemployment can being without work be considered a matter of small significance. As shown in Table 11, one in every three persons unemployed in 1963 had two or more periods of joblessness, and nearly one individual in six had three spells or more. Only a little over a quarter of the unemployed had what might be considered a "minor" amount of time without work, that is four weeks or less, whereas a third were out of work for 15 weeks or more. Nearly two million persons did not find any work during the year.

The long-term unemployed include a sizeable group, perhaps a million persons, who constitute the "hard-core" unemployed. These are men, mostly 35 to 50 years of age, two-thirds of whom have been

Table 11. Extent of Unemployment during 1963.

| Extent of Unemployment | Thousands of Persons | Percentage |
|---|---|---|
| Total unemployed | 14,211 | 100.0 |
| Unemployed 1 to 4 weeks | 3,947 | 27.8 |
| Unemployed 5 to 10 weeks | 2,407 | 16.9 |
| Unemployed 11 to 14 weeks | 1,595 | 11.2 |
| Unemployed 15 to 26 weeks | 2,611 | 18.4 |
| Unemployed 27 weeks or more | 1,840 | 12.9 |
| Did not work but looked for work | 1,811 | 12.7 |
| Total with 2 spells or more of unemployment | 4,635 | 32.6 |
| 2 spells | 2,246 | 15.8 |
| 3 spells or more | 2,389 | 16.8 |

Source: U. S. Bureau of Labor Statistics, "Special Labor Force Report. Work Experience of the Population in 1963," *Monthly Labor Review*, January 1965, p. 8.

engaged on semiskilled or unskilled jobs. Over one-half are Negroes. Only two in five have completed grade school. Their rate of illiteracy is high and their ability to learn new job skills is extremely low. Many have severe psychological problems which limit their ability to cope with the discipline, stresses, and requirement of the workplace.

Of the many millions of persons who experience unemployment, it is the long-term jobless who suffer the greatest deprivation and constitute the most serious social problem. One might include with them those persons whose work histories include frequently repeated spells of joblessness. Not only do these persons suffer the privation, and damage to morale and ability, which result from low income and rejection by society, but so also do their wives and children. In an era of affluence, marked by high incomes, better education, improved nutrition and medical care, good housing, and other benefits, these unfortunate individuals have been denied seats at the banquet table, and because they have been refused, their children also may be rejected; for the education, self-assurance, moral character, and other attributes needed in a society which demands ever more of its workers may not be attainable by the children of unemployment and privation. With the disappearance of the day when anyone could get a job regardless of his or her preparation for work, it becomes vital that society makes sure that every citizen not only is trained to do a job but has a job to do.

# VI

# *Economic Opportunity for All*

"The most elementary fact about prosperity is that you
have to have a job to participate in it."
John Kenneth Galbraith, *The Affluent Society*

MOST OF THE 35 million persons in the United States who live in
poverty[1] glean a niggardly share of America's abundance because of one
major reason: they or the heads of their families do not have good jobs.
Only half of the heads of poor families have jobs at all, while those who
are employed work only intermittently, or part time, or at low wages.

Despite the popularity of dreams about acquiring wealth from a
"killing" on the stock market or an inheritance from a rich uncle,
employment is the main source of income for Americans. Wages and
salaries constitute 70 percent of personal income, and another 10
percent is earned by self-employed persons such as doctors, farmers,
or shop owners. Most of the remaining 20 percent of personal income —
derived from rent, dividends, interest, etc. — is also received by employed or self-employed individuals. Of the over 47 million families
in the United States in 1963, only some 900,000 received incomes of
$3,000 or more exclusively from sources other than employment. For
most Americans there is no path to affluence other than having a good
job.

---

[1] "Poverty" usually is defined as the situation where income is inadequate to meet
basic needs for food, clothing, housing, and other essentials. The amount of income
required for these needs depends, of course, upon such factors as the size of a
family, the ages of its members, place of residence, etc. A family of six obviously
needs more money to make ends meet than an elderly couple. In this discussion,
however, poverty is arbitrarily defined as income of less than $3,000 a year (in 1963
dollars) for a family of two or more persons or $1,500 a year for an individual living
alone. Reasons for use of these criteria are presented in the *Economic Report of the
President,* January 1964, Chapter 2.

Poverty might be considered, therefore, as the result of lack of employment which yields a "living wage." But the relation between employment and poverty is not simply in one direction. Cause and effect work both ways. Poverty is a principal reason why its victims lack qualifications for and opportunities to obtain good jobs. Unemployment (or inadequate employment) and poverty stem from many of the same economic and social conditions.

The nature of unemployment has been discussed at length in this study; here we shall consider its characteristics only as they relate to the problem of poverty.

## ECONOMIC GROWTH AND POVERTY

Economic growth, as has been noted, is considered by many observers as the basic means of providing more employment opportunities. Its role in reducing the proportion of the population afflicted by poverty has been significant. Between 1947 and 1963, median family income (in dollars of constant purchasing power) increased by 48 percent, while the proportion of poor families in the population decreased from 32 to 19 percent. Poverty was reduced, however, by the raising of the incomes of families with wage earners, for total unemployment increased over this period by 1,810,000. The number of poor families without earners grew by almost one million; whereas in 1947 some 16 percent of poor families had no wage earners, 32 percent had no earners in 1963.

Since 68 percent of poor families do include one or more earners, it is evident that continuing economic growth will be extremely important in reducing poverty, as it continues to raise the earnings of employed persons. At the same time, however, the increase in the number and proportion of poor families with no earners is a warning that unemployment as a cause of poverty is becoming more rather than less serious.

In most homes, the head of the family (who is the husband in nine instances out of ten) is the principal breadwinner. Less than half of the heads of poor families were employed and earning an income in 1963. Five percent were unemployed, and 48 percent were not even in the labor force. Only 24 percent of poor families had more than one earner, as compared with the 48 percent of all families which had two or more persons bringing income into the home.

An analysis of the reasons for poverty, therefore, must discover why so small a proportion of the poor are in the job market. Investigation reveals that poverty-stricken individuals can be grouped into three categories: (1) unemployables, (2) persons with limited job qualifications, and (3) children.

The term "unemployables" describes those persons who are prevented from engaging in any remunerative work because of physical or mental disability, responsibility for the care of children or handicapped persons, and similar reasons. It may also embrace older persons who are kept from employment for reasons associated with age.

## DISABILITY AS A BARRIER TO EMPLOYMENT

Physical disability prevents at least two million Americans from working. Many of these individuals are heads of families. While these incapacitated persons may receive insurance or other benefit payments, seldom is this income enough to maintain the family above the poverty level. The individual's condition may require that another member of the family devote considerable time to his care and thus prevent the wife or other relative from taking a full-time job or, indeed, working at all outside the home.

Various programs to aid the disabled and their families are in operation, ranging from direct financial assistance to rehabilitation clinics. In no respect, however, are these programs adequate to reduce significantly the poverty associated with disability. Much more needs to be and could be undertaken to increase job opportunities for the handicapped and to equip them to do useful work. Not only is this true as regards the physically disabled, but also the mentally limited and emotionally disturbed. More adequate nursing facilities, especially publicly operated nursing homes, would free relatives now burdened with the care of the disabled for gainful employment.

## THE ELDERLY POOR

One-third of the nation's poor families are headed by individuals 65 years of age or over. Although this may suggest a picture of the retired worker and his wife struggling to make ends meet on a tiny pension or limited savings, it would be incorrect to assume that age itself is necessarily the cause of poverty among the elderly. Over half of the families headed by persons aged 65 or more have incomes exceeding $3,000 a year.[2] Most elderly poor families have experienced poverty all their lives. Four of every five such families never have attained an annual income of $3,000. The reasons for their poverty, in other words, reach back before these persons entered their sixties or seventies.

---

[2] Among individuals 65 years and older living alone, poverty is more widespread. Well over two and one-half million such persons (62 percent of all) received incomes of less than $1,500 in 1963.

Elderly persons essentially have three possible sources of income: earnings from work, pensions, and income from savings and property. Those persons with more education, better health, and higher skills are the individuals most likely to continue working after 65; they also receive the higher pensions and have the greatest amount of such financial assets as bank accounts, stocks and bonds, real-estate holdings, etc. The pattern of income distribution fashioned by education and work skills in earlier years continues after age 65.

Poverty among the elderly probably will be reduced with the passage of time, as more persons become eligible for pensions under the Social Security Act and private plans, and as a rising level of wages and salaries enables contributions to these pension plans to increase. Rising wages and salaries also will permit the accumulation of more savings and property. Whether the present trend of decreasing labor force participation by those 65 and over[3] will continue or be reversed cannot be predicted. The average length of life has been increasing, thus allowing more years of activity beyond 65. At the same time, educational levels and occupational skill levels are rising — being notably higher among young people than among older people today. These factors, plus improving health, should encourage a rise in labor force participation by older persons. On the other side, however, expanding pension benefits and compulsory retirement plans, plus greater desire for leisure, encourage withdrawal from employment.

## FAMILIES HEADED BY WOMEN

Twenty-six percent of poor families are headed by women. These are families broken up by death of the husband, desertion, separation, or divorce. Nearly half of all the families headed by women are poor, and few of the rest have large incomes. In 1963 the average income of families with a female head was only $3,200, while the average for families with a male head was over $6,500. The necessity of taking care of children[4] or perhaps an invalid parent or other relative prevents some women from performing any work outside the house. Many other female heads of families are able to work only part time. Slightly more than a fourth of female heads of families are year-around full-time workers, compared with over two-thirds of male heads of families.

The pressures of duties in the home is not, however, the only cause of

---

[3] In the past 15 years the labor force participation rate of men aged 65 and over has fallen from over 45 percent to less than 30 percent.

[4] About three out of five families headed by women include children under 18 years of age; nearly one in five includes children under 6 years.

low earnings of families headed by women. Of primary importance is lack of training and skills, which forces women to take low-paying jobs, which frequently offer only part-time employment. Finally, it must be remarked that historically the working woman is still a new phenomenon; most jobs are still reserved for men.[5]

In addition to the disabled, the elderly, and families headed by women, two other groups in American society suffer acutely from the hardships of poverty. They are farm families, 30 to 40 percent of whom are poor, and non-white families and individuals, nearly half of whom live in poverty.

## INCOME OF FARM FAMILIES

The real income of farm families is difficult to measure precisely, since the value of food grown and consumed on the farm, timber cut for fuel, etc., must be added to the family's money income. About 43 percent of farm families, however, received less than $3,000 in money income in 1963. Even if a very generous allowance of $1,000 is made for food and other items supplied by the farm, 28 percent of farm families were poverty-stricken in 1963, as contrasted with 17 percent of non-farm families.

The economic plight of farmers has resulted primarily from the enormous advance which has occurred in the productivity of American agriculture, particularly since World War II. This increase in output per farm worker (which considerably more than doubled between 1947 and 1963) has been brought about by wider use of machinery, feed additives, pesticides, fertilizers, and other technological advances. Fewer farms and farmers are now needed to produce the nation's food supply. Consequently, many farm operators, especially of small farms, have been severely squeezed. They have not had the money to buy new machinery or acquire more land or have lacked the basic education needed to manage their farms efficiently and to put new methods into practice. Caught between low prices for farm products and ever mounting costs, they have been unable to make farming a profitable venture.

Many small farms, especially in Appalachia and other parts of the South, have always been too unproductive, of course, to keep their owners from poverty.

---

[5]Low incomes also characterize women who are not heads of families. Over half of the 6.9 million women living alone in 1963 had incomes of less than $1,500.

## MIGRATION TO THE CITIES

The low income from farming and the decreasing need for farm workers has pushed millions of persons out of agriculture into the cities in search of economic opportunities. The farm population between World War I and World War II numbered about 30 million persons. It has since fallen by about 16 million. Employment in agriculture has declined from over 8 million persons in 1947 to less than 5 million workers today.

This migration from rural areas has aided greatly in reducing the amount of farm poverty. In 1947, 56 percent of farm families had incomes under $3,000 (in 1963 dollars) as compared to 43 percent in 1963. But it is obvious that poverty in rural areas remains a severe problem. Although few farm operators or members of their families show up in the count of the unemployed, it is evident from their low incomes that they are underemployed, that is, not employed up to their productive potential. The extent of unemployment in agriculture shows up clearly among hired farm workers, who averaged only 134 days of farm employment during 1962.

Many farmers and farm workers have turned to other employment, while continuing to remain part-time agricultural workers. Wage rates in small communities in rural areas tend, however, to be low. Furthermore, because of their desire to work only part-time and their lack of training for non-farm occupations, members of farm families are largely restricted to low-skilled, low-paying jobs.

To a distressing extent, the migration of farm people to urban areas has simply meant transfer of the location of poverty, rather than its disappearance. Many such migrants have only vague notions about job opportunities in the city and often have difficulty in finding work. Many are handicapped by inferior education and lack training suitable for non-farm work; typically, their chief resources are a strong back and willing hands. With only limited funds to fall back on while they search for work, they tend to settle in cheap, overcrowded housing in run-down areas of the city. This is especially true of migrants from the South, both whites and non-whites, and of Puerto Ricans.

## THE FUTURE OF FARMING

The future outlook is for a continued decrease in employment opportunities in agriculture. It is estimated that by 1975 less than one out of every twenty American workers will work on a farm, compared with one in fifteen in 1964. Although death and retirement will reduce the ranks of farm owners and workers, the employment problem will become increasingly severe. During the 1960's, 177 rural boys will reach age 20 for each 100 rural men who may be expected to die or retire. Although continued migration will help alleviate the problem, underemployment and poverty will continue to vex rural areas unless remedial action is taken. Two kinds of action are needed: (1) an increase in jobs in non-agricultural industries, particularly in rural areas, and (2) improved educational opportunities and vocational guidance for youth in farm areas.

## The Plight of the Negro

Nowhere is the closeness of the tie between inadequacy of job opportunities and the presence of poverty more clearly and tragically illustrated than in the plight of the Negro. Negroes are victims to a far greater degree than whites of the personal and social disadvantages which produce unemployment, low earnings, and poverty — inferior education, lack of training for skilled jobs, bad health, broken families, a high number of children per family, residence in the South or in the slum areas of large cities. Equally important, however, as reason for the depressed economic situation of Negroes is racial discrimination. This shows most clearly in the fact that where the education, training, and skill of the Negro worker are equal to or even superior to that of the white worker, the Negro's earnings are markedly lower and his risk of being unemployed greater.

The 22 million non-whites in the United States in 1963, over 20 million of whom were Negroes,[6] comprised only 11.7 percent of the population, but they included 21.0 percent of the unemployed and 23.4 percent of the nation's poor families. Forty-three percent of Negro families were poor in 1963, as compared to 16 percent of white families. Average family income for non-whites was $3,500, for whites $6,500.

## Jobs at Which Negroes Work

The unemployment and low pay which are the lot of Negro workers result from the low-skilled jobs to which a large proportion have been restricted. Most of these are jobs traditionally assigned to Negroes or

---

[6]In this discussion the terms "Negro" and "non-white" are used as equivalent. Actually, Negroes comprise 92 percent of the non-white population of the United States: 98 percent in the Southeast, 96 percent in the North Central and Northeast, but less than 50 percent in the West. The other major non-white groups are American Indians, Puerto Ricans, Mexican-Americans, and persons of Asian ancestry. The economic condition of these groups, except the last, resembles that of the Negroes.

ones which white workers are tending to leave because of their declining importance in the economy or the limited prospects they offer for economic advancement. In 1963, nearly 30 percent of employed Negro males worked as unskilled laborers, as contrasted to only 9 percent of white men. Another 25 percent filled semiskilled jobs. Only 15 percent of non-white males had white-collar jobs, as compared to over 40 percent of white men. Negro men seldom are self-employed or occupy managerial positions; less than 2 percent were so engaged in 1963, as compared with 15 percent of white men. Negro men are making some progress in the professional and technical fields, but in 1963 only 3.5 percent worked in these areas, as compared to over 12 percent of white men.

Household service provides the employment for over a third of all female Negro workers, while another 23 percent are engaged in similarly low-paid service jobs in hotels, restaurants, office buildings, and elsewhere. Only 9 percent of Negro women are employed as typists, secretaries, and in other forms of office work, the occupational category which engages one-third of all white female workers.

## NEGRO UNEMPLOYMENT

The average earnings of non-white workers reflect not only the low-status jobs which they fill, but also the extensive unemployment which so many experience. Average earnings of non-white males in 1963 were 57 percent of white males; earnings of non-white females averaged 53 percent of those of whites.

About 900,000 non-white workers were unemployed in 1963. This amounted to one of every ten Negro workers, as compared to an unemployment rate half as large, one in twenty, for white workers. The unemployment rate for Negroes is much higher than for whites in every age and sex group, in every occupation[7] and industry, and in every region of the country.

The unemployment rate for non-white youth is so high that it constitutes a serious social problem. Over 23 percent of teen-age Negro boys and 30 percent of teen-age Negro girls were unemployed in 1964. In contrast, about 14 percent of white teen-agers were out of work. Even in the 20 to 24 year age group, 13 percent of non-white men and 18 percent of the women were unemployed. When one remembers that these are national averages and that unemployment rates among poorly educated Negro youths in slum areas may range as high as 90 percent,

[7]See Table 5.

he reasons for juvenile delinquency, crime, and street riots are not
ard to find.

Not only is the proportion of non-whites who are unemployed high,
out non-whites remain jobless for longer periods than do whites. Also,
hree times as many Negroes as whites can obtain only part-time work
when they do locate jobs.

Over half of adult Negro women are in the labor force, as compared
o two-fifths of white women. Two factors account for this higher
ate of employment. Nearly one Negro family in five is headed by a
woman, while only one white family in thirteen has a female head. This
s the result of a greater frequency of separation, desertion, or death
of the husband in Negro families. Even where the husband is present
n the house, his low earnings and frequent unemployment often make
t necessary for the wife to work. The low earnings of Negro females
year-round full-time workers averaged only $2,280 in 1963) mean that
he family entirely or largely dependent on such earnings is most likely
o live in poverty.

## RACIAL DISCRIMINATION

The unfavorable economic situation of Negroes is caused by more
han a low educational level and other characteristics also shared by
nany white persons. Racial discrimination has barred Negroes from the
oetter jobs in our economy and continues to do so. Not only is the
oroportion of Negro high school and even college graduates employed
n higher-status occupations markedly below the proportion of white
graduates, but also the jobs which Negroes do occupy in these fields
are generally the less remunerative positions. Non-white high school
graduates earn less, on the average, than white workers in the same
occupation who have completed only the eighth grade — in some
nstances as much as a third less. Indeed, census data suggest that the
average non-white man who has completed college can expect to earn
ess during his lifetime than the white man who did not go beyond
he eighth grade.

## EDUCATION AND DISCRIMINATION

Many of the factors producing poverty can be grouped under two
nain headings: (1) inadequate education, and (2) discriminatory hiring
oractices. The significance of education and discriminaton in thwart-
ng economic advance for Negroes has just been discussed. Other large
groups of the poverty-stricken are similarly affected. Older persons
generally have considerably lower amounts of education than the

younger persons in the population, and whatever the accuracy of the view, are considered difficult to train for new jobs. They also find avenues of employment closed for other reasons associated with age. Likewise, women encounter discrimination in hiring because of their sex. While slightly more women than men complete high school, only a small proportion of females go on to college or receive job training equivalent to that of men. Hence, the woman who must support herself or a family finds her employment opportunities restricted to low-paying, often part-time jobs. Farmers, unless Negroes, do not encounter discrimination but do suffer severely from below-average educational attainment. Removal of unjustified discrimination in hiring and expansion of opportunities for education and training must therefore be the basic elements in any "war against poverty."

## Need to Eliminate Slums

Elimination of poverty from American society will involve, however, far more than the elimination of discrimination based on color, age, or sex and the improvement of educational opportunities. It also will require enormous change and improvement in the physical and social environment in which millions of Americans live. Persons crowded into noisy, dirty, living quarters in run-down neighborhoods where the only recreational centers are the tavern or the sidewalks of a busy street, cannot realistically be expected to possess the incentive and opportunity to improve their educational qualifications or to develop the personal attitudes and habits necessary to acquire better jobs. Pessimism, indifference, laziness, and other characteristics which deter self-improvement are the consequence of the hardships imposed by slum conditions. The poor emotional and physical health of many poverty-stricken individuals, which is the result both of the inferior environment in which they live and their lack of access to adequate medical care, is important in causing lack of energy and drive.

If poverty is to be reduced, slum neighborhoods must be replaced by housing adequate for family needs. Recreational facilities, such as playgrounds, parks, and community centers, must be provided. There is urgent need for more and better libraries to provide opportunity for cultural improvement. Health centers and hospitals, treating psychiatric as well as physical illnesses, are necessary, as are programs offering prenatal care of mothers.

## One-Half of the Poor Are Children

The urgency of the need to improve the physical and social environment in which poor families live lies primarily in the fact that one-half

f the nation's poor are children. Some fifteen million youngsters
ace the handicaps imposed by poor diet, crowded living quarters,
nadequate medical care, and exposure to bad social conditions. Unless
hey are provided with a better physical and social environment and
pportunity for education, most of these children will end up, like
heir parents, unequipped to meet the challenges of the modern
conomy and condemned to a lifetime of poverty.

Poor parents are unable to furnish their children with the education
nd other advantages needed to improve their situation. Often they
annot provide even adequate nutrition and medical care. The frustra-
ion and lack of motivation, hope, and incentive in the poverty-
tricken family constitute a barrier to the child's prospects as powerful
s lack of financial means. It is difficult for children to find and follow
aths leading out of poverty in an environment where little oppor-
unity exists, and optimism and hope are smothered by concern with
ay-to-day survival — where is money for the rent coming from, is
here enough to eat, can we afford to call a doctor.

The transmittal of poverty from one generation to the next is
evealed by all sorts of data. A recent study of recipients of government
id to dependent children revealed that 40 percent of the parents in
amilies receiving such welfare grants themselves were raised in homes
vhere public assistance had been received. Another study of poor
amilies disclosed that two-thirds were headed by persons who had
ess than an eighth grade education and that among the children in
hese poor families who had finished school one-third had not gone
eyond the eighth grade. Fewer than half the children in poor families
ad graduated from high school, compared with three-fourths of the
hildren in better-off families.

## EDUCATION: KEY TO THE FUTURE

The future trend of employment opportunities in the United States
s definite and clear. Jobs requiring a high amount of educational
reparation are expanding rapidly; those requiring little or no train-
ng are disappearing. For the majority of jobs today in the American
conomy a high school education or better is required. In a rapidly
ncreasing percentage, a college education is needed. Those lacking
ducation and training are condemned not merely to low-paid tasks;
nany will find little or no work at all available.

Unemployment, as we have seen, has many causes. In the past,
usiness cycles and an inadequate rate of economic growth have been
najor reasons for large-scale joblessness. They may continue to be in

the future, although it is highly likely that wise economic planning by government and business may reduce or eliminate their significance. The other major source of unemployment — lack of education and training — will continue to be a threat to the welfare of millions of Americans until our energies and resources are fully committed to assuring educational opportunities for all persons.

# *Appendix*

## EMPLOYMENT ACT OF 1946, AS AMENDED

### [Public Law 304—79th Congress]

AN ACT To declare a national policy on employment, production, and purchasing power, and for other purposes.
Be it enacted by the Senate and House of Representatives of the United States of America in Congress assembled,

### SHORT TITLE

Section 1. This Act may be cited as the "Employment Act of 1946."

### DECLARATION OF POLICY

Section 2. The Congress declares that it is the continuing policy and responsibility of the Federal Government to use all practicable means consistent with its needs and obligations and other essential considerations of national policy, with the assistance and cooperation of industry, agriculture, labor, and State and local governments, to coordinate and utilize all its plans, functions, and resources for the purpose of creating and maintaining, in a manner calculated to foster and promote free competitive enterprise and the general welfare, conditions under which there will be afforded useful employment opportunities, including self-employment, for those able, willing, and seeking to work, and to promote maximum employment, production, and purchasing power. (15 U. S. C. 1021.)

### ECONOMIC REPORT OF THE PRESIDENT

Section 3. (a) The President shall transmit to the Congress not later than January 20 of each year an economic report (hereinafter called the "Economic Report") setting forth (1) the levels of employment, production, and purchasing power obtaining in the United States and such levels needed to carry out the policy declared in section 2; (2) current and foreseeable trends in the levels of employment, production, and purchasing power; (3) a review of the economic program of the Federal Government and a review of economic conditions affecting employment in the United States or any considerable portion thereof during the preceding year and of their effect upon employment, production, and purchasing

73

power; and (4) a program for carrying out the policy declared in section 2, together with such recommendations for legislation as he may deem necessary or desirable.

(b) The President may transmit from time to time to the Congress report supplementary to the Economic Report, each of which shall include such supplementary or revised recommendations as he may deem necessary or desirable to achieve the policy declared in section 2.

(c) The Economic Report, and all supplementary reports transmitted under subsection (b) of this section, shall, when transmitted to Congress, be referred to the joint committee created by section 5. (15 U. S. C. 1022.)

## COUNCIL OF ECONOMIC ADVISERS
## TO THE PRESIDENT

Section 4. (a) There is created in the Executive Office of the President a Council of Economic Advisers (hereinafter called the "Council"). The Council shall be composed of three members who shall be appointed by the President, by and with the advice and consent of the Senate, and each of whom shall be a person who, as a result of his training, experience, and attainments, is exceptionally qualified to analyze and interpret economic developments, to appraise programs and activities of the Government in the light of the policy declared in section 2, and to formulate and recommend national economic policy to promote employment, production, and purchasing power under free competitive enterprise. The President shall designate one of the members of the Council as Chairman.

(b) The Council is authorized to employ, and fix the compensation of, such specialists and other experts as may be necessary for the carrying out of its functions under this Act, without regard to the civil service laws and the Classification Act of 1949, as amended, and is authorized, subject to the civil service laws, to employ such other officers and employees as may be necessary for carrying out its functions under this Act, and fix their compensation in accordance with the Classification Act of 1949, as amended.

(c) It shall be the duty and function of the Council—

(1) to assist and advise the President in the preparation of the Economic Report;

(2) to gather timely and authoritative information concerning economic developments and economic trends, both current and prospective, to analyze and interpret such information in the light of the policy declared in section 2 for the purpose of determining whether such developments and trends are interfering, or are likely to interfere, with the achievement of such policy, and to compile and submit to the President studies relating to such developments and trends;

(3) to appraise the various programs and activities of the Federal Government in the light of the policy declared in section 2 of this title for the purpose of determining the extent to which such programs and activities are contributing, and the extent to which they are not

74

contributing, to the achievement of such policy and to make recommendations to the President with respect thereto;

(4) to develop and recommend to the President national economic policies to foster and promote free competitive enterprise, to avoid economic fluctuations or to diminish the effects thereof, and to maintain employment, production, and purchasing power.

(5) to make and furnish such studies, reports thereon, and recommendations with respect to matters of Federal economic policy and legislation as the President may request.

(d) The Council shall make an annual report to the President in December of each year.

(e) In exercising its powers, functions, and duties under this Act—

(1) the Council may constitute such advisory committees and may consult with such representatives of industry, agriculture, labor, consumers, State and local governments, and other groups as it deems advisable;

(2) the Council shall, to the fullest extent possible, utilize the services, facilities, and information (including statistical information) of other Government agencies as well as of private research agencies, in order that duplication of effort and expense may be avoided.

(f) To enable the Council to exercise its powers, functions, and duties under this Act, there are authorized to be appropriated such sums as may be necessary.

## JOINT ECONOMIC COMMITTEE

Section 5. (a) There is established a Joint Economic Committee, to be composed of eight Members of the Senate, to be appointed by the President of the Senate, and eight Members of the House of Representatives, to be appointed by the Speaker of the House of Representatives. In each case, the majority party shall be represented by five members and the minority party shall be represented by three members.

(b) It shall be the function of the joint committee—

(1) to make a continuing study of matters relating to the Economic Report;

(2) to study means of coordinating programs in order to further the policy of this Act; and

(3) as a guide to the several committees of the Congress dealing with legislation relating to the Economic Report, not later than March 1, of each year (beginning with the year 1947) to file a report with the Senate and the House of Representatives containing its findings and recommendations with respect to each of the main recommendations made by the President in the Economic Report, and from time to time to make other reports and recommendations to the Senate and House of Representatives as it deems advisable.

(c) Vacancies in the membership of the joint committee shall not affect the power of the remaining members to execute the functions of the joint committee, and shall be filled in the same manner as in the case of the original selection. The joint committee shall select a chairman and a vice chairman from among its members.

(d) The joint committee, or any duly authorized subcommittee thereof is authorized to hold such hearings as it deems advisable, and, within the limitations of its appropriations, the joint committee is empowered to appoint and fix the compensation of such experts, consultants, technicians, and clerical and stenographic assistants, to procure such printing and binding, and to make such expenditures, as it deems necessary and advisable. The cost of stenographic services to report hearings of the joint committee, or any subcommittee thereof, shall not exceed 25 cents per hundred words. The joint committee is authorized to utilize the services, information, and facilities of the departments and establishments of the Government, and also of private research agencies.

(e) There is authorized to be appropriated for each fiscal year, the sum of $125,000 or so much thereof as may be necessary, to carry out the provisions of this Act, to be disbursed by the Secretary of the Senate on vouchers signed by the chairman or vice chairman.

(f) Service of one individual, until the completion of the investigation authorized by Senate Concurrent Resolution 26, 81st Congress, as an attorney or expert for the joint committee, in any business or professional field, on a part-time basis, with or without compensation shall not be considered as service or employment bringing such individual within the provisions of sections 281, 283, or 284 of title 18 of the United States Code, or of any other Federal law imposing restrictions, requirements, or penalties in relation to the employment of persons, the performance of services, or the payment or receipt of compensation in connection with any claim, proceeding, or matter involving the United States. (15 U. S. C. 1024.)

*hat "human relations" factors do workers consider*
  *important?*

*ow do workers judge a "fair" wage?*

*hat can be done to soften the impact of inevitable*
  *industrial change?*

*ow do workers adjust to such a change?*

*hy do workers voluntarily change jobs?*

*ow are secondary schools preparing their pupils*
  *for the labor market?*

# *WORKERS and*
# *INDUSTRIAL CHANGE*

## *By* Leonard P. Adams and Robert L. Aronson

This volume reports these and many other findings from a study and analysis of the experience of Auburn, New York, workers after the shutdown of a major industry. Also included is an analysis of the patterns and process of entry into the job market of the present labor force.

"This book is an addition to our knowledge of labor markets and should be closely read by personnel and employment managers as well as by community relations directors."—*Personnel*

"...will be of value and interest to all students of the labor market, as well as to other social scientists and policy-makers who are concerned with problems of mitigating the human shocks of inevitable industrial change."—HERBERT S. PARNES, *Annals*

Cloth   224 pp.   $3.00

*Order from*

NEW YORK STATE SCHOOL OF INDUSTRIAL AND LABOR RELATIONS, *A Contract College of the State University*, CORNELL UNIVERSITY, ITHACA, NEW YORK

810075

C0-CCP-250

*The Phoenix Living Poets*

—————————

# ABOUT TIME

Poets Published in
The Phoenix Living Poets Series

★

ALEXANDER BAIRD · ALAN BOLD
GEORGE MACKAY BROWN
JENNIFER COUROUCLI
GLORIA EVANS DAVIES
PATRIC DICKINSON · D. J. ENRIGHT
JOHN FULLER · DAVID GILL
J. C. HALL · MOLLY HOLDEN
JOHN HORDER · P. J. KAVANAGH
RICHARD KELL · LAURIE LEE
LAURENCE LERNER
CHRISTOPHER LEVENSON
EDWARD LOWBURY · NORMAN MACCAIG
JAMES MERRILL · RUTH MILLER
LESLIE NORRIS · ROBERT PACK
ARNOLD RATTENBURY
ADRIENNE RICH · JON SILKIN
JON STALLWORTHY
GILLIAN STONEHAM
EDWARD STOREY · TERENCE TILLER
SYDNEY TREMAYNE
LOTTE ZURNDORFER

# ABOUT TIME

*by*

P. J. KAVANAGH

Those whispers just as you have fallen or are
falling asleep – what are they, and whence?

COLERIDGE

CHATTO AND WINDUS

THE HOGARTH PRESS

1970

Published by
Chatto & Windus Ltd
with The Hogarth Press Ltd
42 William IV Street
London WC2

★

Clarke, Irwin & Co Ltd
Toronto

Distributed in the United States of America
by Wesleyan University Press

ISBN: 0-8195-7024-9

57905

© P. J. Kavanagh 1970

Printed in Great Britain by
T. H. Brickell and Son Ltd
The Blackmore Press, Gillingham, Dorset

For my father

# ONE

My father barely believed in the private life.
His cronies were public, at home he mostly slept.
Even his death was in public, nurses wept
Intoning Catholic responses, and the worst
Was that his genuine public smile went first.

During the war, bombed from flat to flat,
My father's religious maxim – "Travel Light":
Six months I oiled, then left behind, an unused cricket bat.
Up on the rack went the lived-out-of suitcases;
Below them the carriage rocked, like a breastful of medals,
      with faces.

A reaction to this is a longing to settle. Not down –
For a place to stay as it was till you return.
A room, a patrolling area, sufficiently your own
To give the illusion of white, vegetable, roots.
But my father's example put green nettles in my boots.

He was right, he was wrong, he was weak, he was strong,
Seeing the funny side (the dog it was that died):
Life – a show on the road, a series of one-night stands:
Doubt – a poison in the colon or an irritation in the glands:
The greatest sin – to spend life sitting on your hands.

No room for windy pretensions, his world was a vast
Gilray cartoon (only kinder), himself as absurd as the rest,
And private matters were not got off, but held close to, the
      chest.
What would you make of me now, mulling a personal past
In public, and in this quiet corner at last?

What would you make of this place? I do not know
And it's too late to matter. So many ways to slow
The spinning world. To move is one. Like mine your vertigo
Needed a balancing pole. But Prospero
Stuck-up on his island with his wand, and Trinculo

Burping in braces, headed for the bar,
Are not so far apart as they appear.
You, preferring donkey-rides at Margate, I prefer
(If you wish) this snobbish separation, like it here
Down eighty muddy steps and miles from nowhere

Travelling Light, in four walls, by a lake
Not even the Green Dragon locals know is here.
No electric light, water from fronded rock
Tasting of caves; food and fuel humped down on the back,
And the few planted flowers nightly eaten by deer.

And this place is an island. Round its shore
Predictable tides slap and suck with drear
Solipsist self-accusations, trying to drag me elsewhere.
Freud, it seems, was right: becoming your own master
You destroy The Father, shovel a way clear

For guilts to multiply like rabbits only faster.
Oedipus-like you mislike the joy of your eyes
In their sudden unfettered seeing – which may be Greek,
Tragic, Freudian, but is also lies.
I didn't come to hide, I came to seek.

First time down the steps we were stopped by a blast
Of orange and flame trombones (last year's beech leaves,
        beech-mast,
Undisturbed by the winds of a year and the rains
Because of the steep of the bank and intertwines
Of the beech-boughs) – this was a place, at last!

As orange trombones blared at us over yew-green
Water under a smoke-blue counterpane
Of warm, eye-level mist beaded with black birds, and, brown,
The last of this year's leaves see-saw'd singly down
Like notes from a musical stave in a film cartoon –

A stone shed in a wood. A place of regraspable fact.
Our lives in the cities seem to become as abstract
As other people's pain on television. We barely meet and never
    give
More than we can afford. We sleep, and dream we live
Down streets through which enormous horrors move

Smiling like aunts . . . Who has never stood in Piccadilly,
Alone, watching the neon time unreel,
And felt more scared, trying not to be silly,
Felt more desolation than a man should feel
Drop like lead and overturn his belly?

. . . You keep me to doggerel, rightly, my Margate-
Preferring father. I hear you sniff and say,
Caring no more for the poet maudit
(Pronounce it to rhyme with "audit") even than I
'Love in a Cottage' for those who can afford it!

Right! But listen to nightsticks of cowparsley quelling a riot
Of lesser herbage. Night and day, winter and summer, listen
In curious shadow, between two oil-lamps, to the quiet
(The sun, we are shadowed by forest, seldom prolongs a visit)
Of the waterfall, like a constantly flushing cistern.

Even if you saw the point (and you might)
Two days of dripping eaves in bottle-green light
And you'd puff, fast, to a bus-stop, to the lights across the
    park.
This is love-in-a-cottage all right.
It's starting again, travelling light, in dark.

9

Hogweed, horsetails, couch-grass, light-starved clematis,
Coal-tits, herons, moorhens, slow-worms – are dramatis
Personae of a mortality play. They make it clear,
Although we seem the star parts, one move from us
Of inattention or condescension and we disappear,

Just stand about looking foolish, looking at nothing,
At trees like green things in the way,
At defined tones of green turned to indefinite grey,
At worlds like Victorian servants doing whatever they're doing,
Kneeling, backs towards us, going away

To leave us, slumped, alone. These things are there.
And whether we are or not they neither know nor care.
To see them is – to see them (I thought moorhens were
Just black, they're different browns and fawns under a sheen)
Is a gift you can lose as though it had never been.

Is a gift . . . Just now I went to the wood to pee.
I'd forgotten the night. The night fell on my face
With a swift, dropping, dark, cold embrace.
An open-mouthed wind, a black, breathing tree,
The moon, the clouds, the muscled boughs were over me

And settled on my shoulders. The heavy night,
Cold as water, dark as a fish, offered me its weight.
You were wrong, my father! We travel heavy, not light.
We must take the whole heaviness, settle our feet on the earth,
Till it pushes us back, like a child through the waters of birth,

With our selves on our shoulders heavy as libraries.
All of our lives are legends, none a mere skewer of days,
But a rhythm of griefs and glimpses, a sequence of pages,
Till stiff with our binding we fall through the last of the
        Stages
Glaired with the green of the world, startled by praise.

Praise for the presences here, like an open secret.
Just now outside in the wood I could almost touch it,
Elastic as bark and sure as roots, stretching and holding fast,
Certain and conscious, rejecting nothing, the past
Never a skin to slough but to wear unencumbered at last.

Neither understanding nor misunderstanding we climb
In dark, tethered to stations our shadows keep.
At night in a hole in the ground under the winds that sweep
Confusion to us all, dogged as Sherpas we climb
Up through a shuttered hole, up through cluttered sleep . . .

An apologia, father, for a flight to a whispering dark,
A hayfoot, strawfoot, clayfoot attempt to grow
Feathers and leaves, a wig of winds. The winds that blow
Us all, blow now to the lights of the park,
Leaves to a shuttered window. Part of the legend also.

# TWO

We move, tall as we like,
towards roods, through cave-runs,
grey, heraldic pillars,
broken, or not.
                    Maned horses
on the skyline
like legends
print themselves black.

Fistfuls of birds on springs,
branched candelabra, thistles,
armorial purples.
                    A stoat
shining with mouse
throats grasses, horsetails
(printed fossils in these walls)
till Jove, a brown cloudburst, warm,
of owl, twitches away the mouse.
Seconds.
Details –

make up legends:
What he said to her: irritations: "No.
Why should I smoke your hash?
It would make me walk
through violet tassels
over the opposite hillside
crying
'Holy willow-herb!'"

God's a tail, a cirrus, whisking
behind, below, away.
I only know
the air
is whitely curled round rain.

Crouched, deaf, in a shed
(black-faced sheep, wigged judges,
stand outside, still,
but my wool has no oil),
knee-high swallows carve
fields for flies.
The way the swallows, flies, shed-roof, use it
is what I know of air.

Sulphur birds in horizons of slate
tumble precisely invisible staves of air. Careful
notes, on a dark sheet.

After so much standing
easy to think of trees
folding back like lids,
pylons moving, to scare crows.

All sleeps and fallings, meannesses,
all waiting for the heavy clock-turn, all
gladnesses,
move inside the legend like slow beasts.

Two came together, make
the legendary child
wet with messages.
Only look at him!
Dries into a man, remains
a legend.

Sermons in stones – don't hear them,
see the stones.
Empty the bag on the hill:
self, stones, inside-weather.
Stand inside

staring,
eyes circled in skull,
child in the arms
or on the arm of a child,
staring in dark at white
ounces of burning birds,
fossils, curled mist, horses,
trees
like bars.
Believing in magic,
coolly.
Until the brown cloudburst.

The world
is logical as cards.
Plays us.
We play,
legendary, blindly, deafly,
deftly. Deaf Gods.
Dear. In magic, printed in white air.

# THREE

The telephone drills into a pool of silence
Calling to London, Dublin, calling away
To a world thought by some to be glamorous, some superficial,
In fact to a trade like any other,
      Neither green nor grey.

A disturbance perhaps? Perhaps. With the nerve of a Blondin
We might stand on the sag of the slack-rope over Niagara
Till the crash and the spume and the yellow boiling below
Came up through the footsoles, entered the head and there was no
      Blondin anymore

But an apotheosis of spray. Perhaps. But as
For the rest of us Blondin's balancing act
Lands back on crowded banks, his diamond tights
Spangled with drying splashes. We can never stand quite
      Still, in fact

Air is not for standing. Water falls
Because it has to from a high place to a low.
As telephones remind, we are not still.
The going of water is white and noisy and it's
      A glorious way to go.

But doubts resound, rebound. Given one moment longer
Poised between bird and water, what might we see?
Basso spiders singing of constellations,
Clear formulations, bright as laundry, hung
      From mouth to tree?

Shapes, colours, cloud-movements, seem to be mouthing
Relaxed languages we can almost hear.
A man is caught between two voices, theirs
Which call to fall to join them, and his own, which makes
      A separation clear.

. . . Corridors of whispers like old songs.
Each man has a headful. Calls he hears in sleep.
A man remembers loves more real than he is, old errors
Haunt him like catarrhs, and promises
        He cannot keep.

He calls his friends, the dead he falls to join!
They tug him on through their magnetic field.
In hosts they dandle him, blow on him like a dandelion,
Up the M1 or to Paddington, anywhere, whisperers
        Everywhere concealed.

The ground of the past is stringing with trip-flares, gossamers.
And the living entangle him in a web of fact!
Each is as real as the other! Dizzy, he tries to name things,
Asserts his toes touch pavement, slack-rope, grass,
        That he's not abstract,

Like stars he keeps a sprained geometry; like clouds,
Busy as bats, dark and quick, or white and slow,
Depending on elsewhere pressures – smudges, cauliflowers –
Not minding it seems to be either or other, being
        Clouds is what they know.

He watches the ousel, white-bibbed like a waiter,
Like a blackbird with a piece of bread in its beak,
Flying, be true to the water, curve where the water
Curves, precisely keep the crooked line
        The waters take.

Hears trees in the wind at night each making a different sound.
Beeches that hiss like straw on fire, elms that creak, cracked
They shed soft burnables, ash like an old man groans,
Tomorrow may fall entirely. At night in dark and wind each tree
        Asserts its fact.

Of these he takes to town a pantechnicon! As Cowper
Sliced carrots for his hare with shaking hand
He keeps him upright on a rope of winds
With details, small affections carefully performed. Ceremonious
      The balance of the mind.

To hold himself, a present, to the sky,
To offer up his being in a bowl, a crumb of life,
Is good. Is best. Is dangerous. It is to stand
With cold and tender feet a rope he cannot see,
      To walk a knife

Between two darks and a hundred selves all whirring
Like ill-made gyroscopes. No wonder Cowper's hand shook.
But if his feeding Tiney "surliest of his kind"
Kept Cowper whole, in patches, that was not
      His luck, but work.

So we work on and down. Ploughland, Oxford Street,
The journey's one and interim. Driving a furniture van
Of unsystem'd adhesions, of holds we rummage among
For selves we belong to, searching to be human. And the work
      Not soon done.

AT-B

# FOUR

What is he looking for, crossing seas
to sweat in bars with friends and enemies, leant back
with nothing to say much, under a poisonous pink
too-high vault enskying self and drink, what does he think,
    standing relieved in the alley saluting Jupiter,
the black Dublin sky over his cheek
    like silk, what does he think he is looking for?

What does he find? Presumably what he's after:
sooner or later someone warms her shoes
by crossing floors towards him, in her hand
a kind of rescue, two tickets to Dreamland.
    He brushes rouge-marks of the seat from his behind . . .
Our lives could be called simple if they choose
    only old answers to old questions, round and round.

Used tickets in his pockets, in the park at Easter
a distant figure shields her eyes like one he knew;
the East Cheam Junior Brass Band blowing hot
"Colonel Bogey", drummer three feet high – now what
    in those two sights behind his sunglasses stings his eyes wet?
Old emotions that obstruct his view.
    His feet, turned back to find them, fail, and sweat.

*

That's not the whole of it. Ask again.
If he wakes in the morning with a memory of pain
(Not of his own, of someone else's), wakes in sweat,
If he refuses to make his mind go shut
On that audible whisper, is he enjoying it?
If he pulls out prettier snaps of days,
When they were all, when it was all so long ago –
What is he doing to now – to time, and place?
What is he punishing? He would like to know.

When he has walked as far as he could up a dead-
End, with nothing, hardly anything, in his head
And nothing in his eyes but two cold shoes
And they're still not empty after years,
What, when he uses the tricks that most of us use,
That make up most of our lives – hairs
Of the sex that bit him, action, drink –
What, if he's still thinking, is he sensibly to think?
That he has a grief to bear, like yours?

Some muscular mornings that seems adequate.
But now in the park and often he can hear
Garbled talk-back from the Great Broadcaster,
Who is nowhere, in the cortex, or above the bands of Easter,
Booming something he can't fathom quite and where
On earth should he be now instead of dragging about
A twangling park with a broken radio set
Not quite receiving not-quite-messages that sting his eyes wet,
Walking, walking, till he's worn his own disgusting shoes out?

\*

There must be something cool to stand on.

Children run towards an ice-cream van.
They come from nowhere, all South London
houses, nearly all, are down.
The van is playing, like a xylophone,
a half a mile of corrugated iron.

There must be something, or let's all fall in.

The heart leaps up when it beholds
Price's Candleworks in greys and golds
in thin, tin light.
Its chimney's split apart

like galvanised tin thighs.
It has to rise,
the heart. Like fish on flies
it lives on what it sees.
Tower blocks.
Tower blocks.
Groups of blacks,
sun still in their turnups,
teeth whiter than the flesh of turnips.
A wind between the towers
lifts old newspapers:
TOWER BLOCK FALLS DOWN.
RACIST . . . FASCIST . . .
                                Politics is
everything, is skin, is houses.
He finds his own. He shuts it. Pays his taxes.
Keeps a wife and child. At any rate
he lives with them. And they with him.
                                The State
by no means withers away. Perhaps he does . . .
But no.
            The wife, the he, the child are dynamos
driven by merely living, driven on
humming, dreaming, through the streets of iron,
which are no man's, every man's a room
hung inconsequential as an album.
He stands in his and has

what seems the first illumination his.

Despair is shoes of iron
not to be feared.
On, are cool; on rock
of merely living hold upright.

A childhood candle he snuffs out.
Days were sepia by the light it gave.
Outside, the day acquires a nearer look.
Surprised, he tries his feet.

Warm and white inside the shoes they move.

# FIVE

Despair as the beginning of belief? A doctrine out of fashion
        with an activist generation,
understandably – what has their faith ever done for the poor
        but institutionalise despair?
But – it's hard to believe any more in Rational Man.
        True, we no longer have public execution,
we watch it in comfort on the television.
        True, we're the boss of a few of our germs,
the nastiest ones we bottle and multiply
        against a rainy day.
True, if we have a piece of ourselves cut away
        it happens under ether;
that more nowadays are protected from tangible harms.
        Others we've given novel ways to die.
True we no longer throw on the streets the broken and old,
        we leave them to half-die in half-cold.
Nevertheless – better to live in the twentieth century
        than any brutal other.
At least we've noticed we're running out of solutions,
        noticed the babies floating away
in the thrown-away ablutions, our lunatic tendency to Either/Or
        either Heart or Head,
God or Man, Chastity/Bed, even – Alive/Dead.
        Which brings us back to despair.
Despair, which can make the world die on us, make us take
        the whole bottle of pills,
or prick our arms with dreams we drown inside,
        seems, like a suicide note, the will's
pathetic attempt to punish the world, or another person.
        If one of us can decide
after pro and con (with never a spiteful one)
        to hand his ticket in,
we call him that god-like man, a genuine suicide.

Grant him the admiration
reserved for perfect detachment, like Schopenhauer's,
            envying such composure (although we find
S. kicked his female servant down the stairs
            and having crippled her spent years
trying not to pay her compensation):
            That graceful, negative stances of the mind,
with the normal sublunary tics go hand in hand.

How, then, despair?
                        There's a longer-living kind
            known to everyone over thirty-five.
When early motors begin to gag and rumble,
            and hopes like cookies crumble,
when flogging sex is flogging a hard-mouthed horse
            (pleasant enough), when being alive
is to know that tomorrow will not be better but probably worse.
            And we plead for a shot of love.

But – suppose that love is neither here nor there; like weather,
            whether we notice it
or don't, is everywhere. And we're insisting blue Aegean heat
            is weather, and everything else is not.
Perhaps a particular love becomes everything jumbled together:
            hot marsh mists, sleet,
ice-routines, mirages that curl the heart, tear-monsoons
            and, worst, small unremitting rains.
And love is something we worry too much about
            and none of us lives without
however starved we feel – because we can't. A piece of string
            in the pocket, a favourite itch,
can furnish a moment, a moment of living, rich
            with layered compost,
piled with past, and the present, million movements. There's luck
            in an open eyelid.

Outside, the world like a foreign language waits to be given back
        meaning it never lost . . .
Though truncheons fall like stone snow. Although for thanks
        the generosities are met by tanks
and manacles and murders are the currency
        they've been in every bloody century,
life waits to twist its many shapes, we feel it happen,
        a twitch in the gut,
joy, at an idea or an apple, shaped, misshapen
        sometimes beyond recognition,
surprising a self we thought had to do without it.
        So why should not
(though hints slip through our fingers like wet soap
        seemingly gone for good;
how, when we've never had it, can a hope
        die on us which we've never understood?)
this stiffening-up, this sense of loss, be the definition,
        be love, locked inside-out?

Some see the world as a kind of examination
        with despair as one of the questions.
Youth fills one side of the sheet with spry suggestions.
        Later, on the other,
the writing should be firmer, the words few, harder,
        until with a rattle of breath
and a click of false-teeth we hand it in to whatever
        lies on the other side of death.
Now, speaking as one who's been taught not to ask
        an impossible question
in public, like "Why are we here?"
        but privately asks it like everyone
else – the concept of test, quest, the exam idea,
        though impossible to defend,
seeming to shrink our heads to school-cap size
        in a school of pointless rule –

why does a phrase of Keats' – "The world is a vale
          of soulmaking" – always surprise
a simple agreement? Perhaps it's as well and about time
          to stand and answer my name.
I believe there are holes in the sky. Believe the dead
          real as radio-waves outside my head.
Have dreamed a spiral to a perfect air.
          And I believe in hell.
In confirmation of deprivation. I can fail.
          Not all is well.
I believe, probably from fear (fear of Nothing
          is not a bad idea),
believe in despair, in the deprived, passionate heart,
          where snakes, and ladders, start.

## SIX

Experience we shared
wears through, like clothes.

You move, I know, about your own affairs.

And I have news.
Our friend is in the garden of the mad.
Brown seed-bags on the ash tree – he sees bats.
Coloured robes and Woolworth bells
and Myshkin hairs.
Disturbances
like cooking smells
climb stairs.
Policemen rot the doorbells in the night.

You in a long black 'Fifties coat
(such an old snap-shot)
are present in the hall.
Shake neither head nor finger.
Smile.
Your freedom can contain this.
I remain.
I do not know what best to do,
watched by you.

I climb.
The garden yelp
disturbs the stairs.
I hold the banister.
I cannot help.

I climb into a corner of my brain.
I serve
I swerve
the prison sentence of our counterpane.

Undrugged, the room stays dark.

Bats stay seed-bags in the junkie park.


*


Too many deaths,
too many absences,
pare down.

Downstairs they're turning on.
Visions clatter from their gramophone.
Like chocolate
they eat the eating night,
turning it to fleshy substances.
Why should they not?

Bare trees stare outward into distances.

Upstairs
the room
is hunching shoulders
round its chill.
Understanding circles to the ceiling-light.
Then the roof slides shut.

Below, the desperate
defy the night.
They mingle breaths.

Upstairs the room examines it.

"Come down!"

The room hugs silence like a sound.

"Not yet."
Too many absences to listen at.

Below
eye bores into eye:
"Is this me?"

 Upstairs the room
pushes beyond its station and its name
between two breaths
it balances –
it calls
its deaths like birds into its branches.

## SEVEN

*Retreat upon retreat*
*to find a ground*
*for feet and mind.*
*Though mind sees part*

*of mind, like body, elsewhere.*
*Feet down there.*
*Indifferent observer*
*with an ice balaclava.*

*Mind, which has gone circular,*
*says: "For once, old soldier,*
*I'll do the watching. You*
*try taking over."*

*

*"Perhaps the only part of me,*
*after all, worth love,*
*is him, all clown.*
*He pulls my high-reach down.*

*After all*
*he is the one*
*who takes the pain*
*and just plods on*

*So rubber-faced the rain*
*takes time to reach his chin*
*down the folds of his endurance*
*out and in."*

White having fallen in flakes of Lux,
morning of mists, variously dun.
Albert seated in the birdless wood.
The only white remaining

is on hummocks.
He's beginning again.
The world is neither warm nor cold,
like Albert, who feels nothing.

Having given up trying.
Notices drops of thaw
honestly rolled to the bottom of where they are.
The only bright thing.

*

Is it dead February
or dead December?
Albert
cares not to remember.

Clocks hurt him.
Wives, Albert, wars,
poke elbows at his dream:
"Hey . . . what time?"

He says "OK OK"
climbing out of head.
Does badly (rudely) outside.
Gratefully climbs back, "Where were we . . ."

Not Pierrot. Pierrot of the moon
perhaps. Not Pantaloon,
just Albert (call him) gulping his absurd
like moon-dust, like promise.

Bores him, self-disgust.
Of all he feels, the most is dross.
He never pans it.
Drinks it all.

Memory leads him.
Did it seem?
Not, he thinks. He knows he knows not
which rich seam.

*

Today he's angry. Someone took
negligently
his last cigarette.
Reactionary Albert.

Dislikes his anger. Feels it.
In sofa-corner sits, sulks, and dumb.
Hearing heads of flowers
(tended by someone, not no one)

flinching, like snails.
While to the Liberty drum
over the world's flowerbeds
Freedom fascists come.

That sofa's not his own.
Nothing is. But the past
covers it, not chintz, not tatters.
Is not seen

admittedly. "Can you not see . . .?"
Not bayonets he minds,
ransacking stuffing, horse-hair.
Not loss of anything.

Nothing is quite there.
He gasps, though, airless.
It is the sureness
of the blind bayoneteer!

\*

*Saigon pays fourteen pounds for dead
civilians over eighteen. Seven pounds the rest.*
Albert on bus top turns to the next column.
To love the world outside he does his best.

*Pop-singer's Twenty-first in Chamber of Horrors.
Her cake a cast in icing of her feet.*
Two eyes turned frankly on it could invest
even this world with beauties he's not quite forgotten.

His own, like King's Road buses, cannot move
past a new boutique called "God is Love".
"Christ!" He kneels before his memories, "Forgive
a man who has been blessed who can't bless this."

A glass of wine, a glass, another glass.
Outside, the London afternoon is brass.
He holes out in a bookshop, sees the walls
Are hung with photographs of naked girls

with naked men, and girls with girls
also. Some girls alone
have breasts with ropes on, pulled, cruelly, at.
Their faces, close-up, act, or are in, pain.

He kneels, a knight of Eros, in the shrine.
Perhaps that pain is softness, inside out?
"Can I help you sir?" He sighs Alas.
Inside his flesh he would live always but.

*

It floats away, even the truest book
of lovers true/untrue, of crimes and couplings
and all that, once, he cared intently for.
Too known, that tunnel, further to explore.

He stares at green on unmoved stones in water,
and rooted red also, close-to, symmetrical,
the outside wall of Brixton Methodist Chapel.
The splendid ball also that swings to smash it.

The innocence of things (an old religion).
Other times, other innocencies. Underground
constructed pages flap back down the tunnel:
tube-train faces, washed in air, like pebbles, are his own.

57905

Glimmerings and decays.
Now Albert only sees himself
in D. H. Evans' window.
His face a time-scape in a camera obscura

that includes the future
(at the edge therefore
himself no longer there).
Not good – feels something move

– finds a Gents in Holborn
with plumbing like a monsoon
and a macintoshed city love-guardian
eternally peeing policeman.

*

He doesn't know what yellow stars the path.
Pain has names sometime – joy has too.
Which comes. He stops and shoves his nose
inside a pink-white hedge, white elder, pink dogrose.

The air inside – a sauna bath!
Colour, smell, nothing can change; not news,
not dead greenfinch sticking to the tar.
"Pain and joy are only inside-weather.

"Like Hardy, leant upon a coppice gate,
I'll take and break an old thermometer.
Not hot nor chill can I avoid or choose.
One comes sometimes, sometimes" he shakes the gate "the
                                                    other goes".

(Days pile on.)
Addresses infant son.
"Three times a day you're fed a meal.
Three years

before you remember one.      ·
Your life's a dream of growing.
"Cheers" he lifts his cup
"so's mine.

"You know – I like you. Our every ill
comes not so much from never sitting still
as from dreaming we are woken up."
His son observes the words, like noises snowing.

*

He breathes – the air!
"My dears – I wish you well. I wish
you well – but stand away from me,
an empty dish. And no,

"not cruel. See the sky
fill the empty tree.
I am full.
I am what I have. No more. No

"more. The sky is wine –
it washes. Oh – the air –
I am a back
I follow through a door."

## EIGHT

Car, arrived in shed, disturbs the wren.
A life of movement. And a life of silence.
Wren gone, the car cools, ticks. The shed drips.

As to an aeroplane a tunnel clips.
Darkness aware of green. Trees lead down
Aisles of birds asleep in rows.

Under a ceiling scratched and earthed by boughs –
Circuits of silence. A tuning-in
To batteries of birds. Some valves unclose.

Radar of the night now pings with echoes.
Now is the time for winging-in of ghosts.
Two feet in muddy suede. A dying fire.

*These soles have stood in galleries and bars,*
*Int rains and in urinals (where a man*
*Walked on his heels, a penguin, keeping clean).*

*He thinks: a dying bed goes still, the scene*
*(Not a second and the trolley clangs)*
*An aviary of sympathetic aprons.*

*Blurring the outline of the pointed stone,*
*Silence, these ghosts fly in to feed on,*
*Furling warm wings round . . .*

Breath poises in the ribcage. Silence swells: a sound
Of vaulted halls flurried above with birds
In and out a high bright window.

Cups and the table, feet, below in shadow,
Fall like feathers to their inward weight.
Coloured ghosts, sparks, stir up the air.

The room's unstartled by a glowing chair.
Attention settles like a flock of birds, shapes,
The way a scarf shapes thrown upon a bed.

"Come in, ghosts! if this silence is your bread!"
Life is so prodigal. Devoted now to white
Swan silences it still wholly lives . .

The window catches sparrows bright as olives,
Luminous against an obscure dawn;
Winter grass with yellow in its beak

Suspended, powdering, mote-like
Towards the arched swords, shining, of the dead,
The friendly marriage-swords, the lonely things

Of God. (Mere grasses, starling
Picked-between, and boiling wren.) Wet pigeons' wings
Beat deeply, frightened, in the moist white air . . .

*Cold. A dying fire.*
*Returning random weightlessness again.*
*Grey seagulls quarrelling in tractor-light*

*Morning. Eyes gone skin-tight.*
*Drinking. Nude dreams over the cider-butt.*
*Engines pumping. Rolling. On and on.*

*White face in the cockpit. Contact gone.*
*"Can't stop moving. Engine. Cannot hear you."*
*Crash on silence. Useless stubs of penguin wings.*

Latent light in circles round fence-posts, in rings
Of algae patience. Our light. Distant silences
Still sonorous with new arrivings.

## NINE

The fire is out. The fire has to be relaid.
So, up the bank in the wind. Dipper curves the lake,
cries a radar bleep like an audible bat.
        Against dark
its plumage vanishes, the white blob on its throat,
alone, floats faster than a ping-pong ball.
It stops on a half-sunk bough, dips, lives anxiously locked
        behind the waterfall.
The wood's crosshatched with fallen timber. Smells
of deaths, bird-droppings, mice, white spongy weed-roots.
Sweats, cracks; then – still as a graveyard.
        Some timber, fallen, rots,
turns to water, you tell by the sound and feel
of a boot-kick, smell. Earth sucks it back.
Other goes heavy, hard, weighs into itself.
        Sodden, black,
mud-encrusted, smelling of earthworms, beech is best.
Sawn, is neat, compacted, white inside,
burns slowly, making whitest ash.
        The wood . . .
To enter the wood is like walking into a bottle.
Thin low weeds throw globe shadows of green,
balloons of green balancing greys and brown.
        In between,
thinly, are paths of precise deer.
A tunneller heaves on its back a line of sog.
Tree-creepers pick at crevices, vertical mice.
        A perfect log –
beech – a liftable length. Pivot on thinner end
cracking through kindling, stamping dogmercury juice
shoulder in balancing place and – up.
        A sluice
down slithering mudbanks, collar collecting woodlice,
slaloming conifers, not to wedge the tail.

Fifteen feet long, nine inches across, rested at last
                on the bank-rail.
Gasping, knees bent like a coolie's, clapped
by two-year old from the cottage (he can't understand
why his applause is soundless, ball of thumb
                on heel of hand,
elbows too close to side) . . . Describe. Describe
this ringing, glass-rim noise, a tongueless bell
we seem inside, while moments hit the side of it like rain
                and real rains fall . . .
Things stand around like sentinels, like bells with flame-tongues –
there's flame inside the curry-coloured hare –
swinging in green between trees creaking, falling.
                Guarding where?
These oddly burning things do not seem traps. Human skins
measure the wind, human watering eyes and listenings –
while thin suns circle trees. We may
                be saved by things.
Ears swivel like deer's, like radar-saucers.
What do we, listening (should we listen) hear?
*Where? What fire? What is this talking about?*
                Real shadow-theatre!
Space hangs burning, moments drown in it, Furies dragging
memories through ice; then, in ice, a grey
armpit stain of thaw: warm, underground waters. Glimmerings
                and decay.
We are separate. We spiral up, like grasses, never join.
Each point of a blade, it seems, is meant to take
soundings of air, fire-eater, that it breathes;
                and not mistake
deaf ears for no sound. Sociable as a hayfield!
Or ships in ice, by lamp keeping station,
(signals through dark, jokes, formal as kisses through a grid),
                convoys of separation!
Faces pouched with freight of an unseen
that lives in the hold whether we wish or no.

39

Perhaps a white arrival? Triumphant shouts made echoless
        by endless snow.
On. That coast is no coast. Ice. Love
is the hug of a thermos'd anorak, it shows
as destinations, sweeps of furtherness. A brotherhood
        of ice-floes!

"Domesticities – the finest earth can show"
(said Cowper) never, nobly, quite enough – fine though.
A touch of seedless air burns through those furs.
        But make the fire.
Under the tongueless bell the place stares.
To show one's love before it slips away!
To catch at a place and hold this
        scraping tree,
this dark, this damp smell on the dark stair,
this half-moon window, bag for a whole wind: a caul
shadowed with lamps, and hands, a child's shoe . . .
        Outside the wall
a wind that can kill a man, fling trees down,
makes fire smoke, makes eyes sting that stare
for fire hanging, tongues, in bells of air.

# TEN

Fleeing from colleagues to The Versailles
      Restaurant, Queen's Hotel, Leeds,
alone in a corner in splendour, it's difficult
      after four glasses of solitary wine
to keep one's lips still when one's talking
      to the other, empty, chair.
This room is a dream of a shared palace;
      even three shallow steps
for entrancing down; warmly breathing money
      drifts up an arras,
behind it a Polish waiter draws on a butt
      and rests his face.
Outside, sharp, blind buildings
      slice wind into streets,
people like sticks angle their faces away
      from sodium lighting,
whittled by winds and horrible architecture.

      You'll be a matchstick too,
blown down flues of cities, striding adjacent moors
      in John Buchan rain,
still a dry mannikin, making macintoshed gestures,
      the future crammed with you.
Tonight I'll call you eighteen, adding sixteen
      years, me fifty-three,
your dad pop pater father
      with broken veins in his nose
etcetera. "I've called you here"
      (I cannot believe
this wine is mine and so I drink it, addressing
      an empty chair
in an absurd corner of an unknown city)
      "to thank you."
Your not being here but asleep
      in a dripping wood

with vats of mothers' honey still to tap
    makes it easier
to thank you. "Thank you.
    Merely by being
you showed me valves of the heart
    still pumped, like gills.
And may the same happen to you whatever
    the reason."
           You've laced
your fingers between your knees, your head
    bends over your plate
with an awkward adolescent hairfall.
    I'll never say this.
Or insist how little of me, your age, has changed
    except for outwards;
how invisibly little the drip affects the limestone
    cave-runs we look out from.
Of course not. In sixteen years I'll spare you that;
    a buff, embarassed, with his son.
A shame in some ways. "I loved you so much – how
    you astonished me!
you made me – you made me think again."
    Dreadful! How could you endure it?
Begin again:
           "I ought,
Being so much older, and your father,
    to say something
about life and how to live it. Well –
    It's a series of beginnings.
Beginnings again, from beginnings, like a river.
    That's it! A mortal
Again and Again!"
           Ash is scattered
    over the clover-shaped
butter-pats – I smudge them trying to clean them:
    the nearest foursome

is angled as though in a wind, trying to listen.)
                    "Listen. You
were a new beginning. So
                    you owe me nothing!"

Soils, shafts, ancient geologies dictate
                    the unstraight course of a river.
I shall never know anything of your turnings.
                    You were one of mine.

Small rocks, uprooted flowers, dead birds,
                    we carry with us, grit,
detergent, dying fish. Too big
                    a blockage and unashamed
we shoulder back (we should), right-angle, shrink,
                    expand; find ways round. Stopped
once and for all, we dreadfully explode. Niagara.
                    Underneath us float
rooted, wafting greens, Ophelia's hair.

                    You sprained my flow
into a fresher landscape. Or rather, same old greens,
                    different water.

Starvations, tortures, manacles
                    are facts we
force a way through (and do not speak of here, art
                    can't deal with it,
can't breathe Cyklon B – don't try. Art exists
                    face to face with its
antithesis; defies, defines its opposite)
                    These facts are forms
of fear. Are doomed attempts to stick
                    too long
behind the shelter-rock of one idea.
                    It brings such dooms in wake –
the flow refused – such burstings out!

Would I then not build?
I would not dredge a stream,
        would not murder weeds
more sure of place than we are, would not move
        until I had permission from the air.
The world's a language that we think
        we only speak
when we decline it harshly. Everything is breathing.
        We only think
we think we do not hear.
        This room, like water's breathing.
The cold stones of the city, hear them hawk!
        We are passengers
of our own misting breaths. We two, the same!
        Although I am your father,
you, my son . . .
                "Have I been silent long?"
        My boiled eyes
scour the room.


        Sex? I've thought
of not much else for years and yet I've
        not much to report.
Let it take you down the estuaries of silt
        until you see
perspectives of horizons poised like birds.
        Listen
to the weir below your ribs.
        Listen to the fear
in dirty jokes. Hear the laughter
        also. Oh my dear
how can I know if you'll have the hands of a juggler,
        able to keep
light and dark in the air at once and not
        go boss-eyed! How can I know
you'll have the heart!

You're not
listening and I
have not spoken. Your father
and his father
do not, did not, know.

"Do not believe
anything anyone tells you."
I have you now of course. You lift your head
and grin (and hearts
can nearly burst with unimpartable information:
That we're the same,
brothers, twins, your species, you're not new!)

Calm. There's a journey to be gone
by focussing on the table-cloth: there's flax
there's yellow straw
below wet stars, there's sleep, where opposites
collide, sometimes become
old, slept-in, laundered linen bed-sheets
soft on limbs as water.
Though when we wake we've grown nothing but whiskers,
where were we then?
How dared we dream of carelessness when selves
shrink to pin men
on a railway platform left behind,
the world
fronding out towards us like a fan,
movement and counter-movement,
gathering tighter, clearer?
"Waiter!

Well—
I won't keep you. Be off to your party."
  I want you
to be wholly alive, which is to say
    to be good. "Be good."

Is there a party? Perhaps you only invent one,
    wanting to hug a self-hood,
a mystery, feeling it form
    a calyx round your bud.
Will you one day be able to give it
    to someone? Will there be one
or merely be too many?
    Will the world one day
for you, as at times it astonished your father
    (you helped him)
be open-mouthed, and breathe?
    Will you hear it?
Or will your bud
    nipped by yourself, or broken
by such easy mistimings, fate, or character,
    whirl in a pool of cold,
blackened, embittering the water?
    We all need
such luck . . .
        I catch your shifty grin.
    "Good night." You turn your head.

I watch you watch your father
    go half-drunk to bed.

57905

PR
6061
A9
A64

KAVANAGH, PATRICK
    ABOUT TIME.

**DATE DUE**

GAYLORD                                    PRINTED IN U.S.A.